STRUCTURED

ADOLESCENT

PSYCHOTHERAPY

GROUPS

Billie Farmer Corder, EdD

Professional Resource Press
Sarasota, FL

Published by Professional Resource Press
(An Imprint of Professional Resource Exchange, Inc.)
Post Office Box 15560
Sarasota, FL 34277-1560

The copy editor for this book was Patricia Hammond, the managing editor was Debbie Fink, the production coordinator was Laurie Girsch, and Jami's Graphic Design created the cover.

Library of Congress Cataloging-in-Publication Data

Corder, Billie Farmer, date.
    Structured adolescent psychotherapy groups / Billie Farmer Corder.
       p.   cm.
    Includes bibliographical references and index.
    ISBN 0-943158-74-5
       1. Group psychotherapy for teenagers--Handbooks, manuals, etc.
    I. Title
    RJ505.G7C67   1994
    616.89'152--dc20   93-44822
                                        CIP

DEDICATION

This book is dedicated with love and gratitude to my husband, Bob Corder, who has been my family, friend, and coworker for all these years. He has enriched my life and made this book, and my work, possible.

ACKNOWLEDGEMENT

I would like to express my gratitude and appreciation to my family, Bob Corder, Lucy and Kenney Farmer, and Jean Farmer McCarthy, and to my extended family, particularly Zilla and Raymond Hawkins, Hilary Farmer Tedford, and Jeff H. Farmer, for their support and understanding. I am grateful to my special friends, Betty Varner, Michael Alperin and his family, Marge and John Paulsen, and Carole Sterett for the pleasure and meaning of their true friendship.

I thank my long-time co-worker, Reid Whiteside, for the invaluable contribution he has made to our shared work and Dr. Tom Haizlip and the entire staff of the Child Psychiatry Program of Dorothea Dix Hospital for their assistance and encouragement over the years. I appreciate the assistance of Dr. Ted May, a great teacher, during my early career, and the help of Dr. Michael Rutter, who generously shared his knowledge on several research projects. The support of a generous research grant from the Burroughs Wellcome Research Foundation is gratefully acknowledged. My thanks also to Dr. Peter A. Keller for his editorial assistance and to Debra Fink, Laurie Girsch, and Patricia Hammond of Professional Resource Press for their help in preparing this manuscript for publication.

TABLE OF CONTENTS

INTRODUCTION

This book is a distillation of research and clinical work with adolescent psychotherapy groups which spans 28 years. During these years, I have held groups in state mental hospitals, juvenile court centers, mental health centers, group homes, outpatient clinics, and in private practice. This book concentrates on methods that I have developed with co-workers for structuring the group process, and which have been effective with a large range of youths in varied settings. These methods are based on some of the research described in this book, including our study on curative factors in adolescent psychotherapy groups.

Planning and attention to administrative details and aspects of the co-therapy relationship are critical to the functioning of any psychotherapy group. In addition to these issues, therapy contracts, general legal concerns, and liaison work with parents and agencies are addressed. Chapter 12 describes techniques and procedures for a time-limited, structured psychotherapy group with sexually abused young adolescents. This has been included as an example of a highly structured group approach, and because of the special problems these young victims may present.

STRUCTURED

ADOLESCENT

PSYCHOTHERAPY

GROUPS

1

THEORETICAL APPROACHES TO ADOLESCENT GROUPS

The special advantages of group therapy for adolescents, either alone or as part of a multimodal approach, appear rooted in the relationship of group functions to the typically described tasks of adolescence. For example, groups offer opportunities for development of peer attachments and empathy with others. Groups also offer some perceived protection by the group from a therapist's adult domination as the adolescent struggles toward independence from parental authority. In addition, the group provides a safe environment for adolescents to give and receive peer feedback concerning identity issues, life goals, and relationships with others.

Although the primary purpose of this book is to describe practical strategies for planning and leading adolescent psychotherapy groups, the novice reader may find it useful to review some basic assumptions of different theoretical approaches to adolescent groups. This chapter summarizes several relevant theoretical perspectives.

PSYCHOANALYTICALLY ORIENTED IDENTITY GROUP THERAPY WITH ADOLESCENTS

Rachman (1975) views some dysfunctional adolescents as struggling unsuccessfully with intense identity confusion.

These adolescents lack the necessary skills for effectively developing their capacities for intimacy, inner continuity, and a sense of self. Identity group psychotherapy provides opportunities for positive peer identification. The group members can learn to explore, interpret, and develop insight into their identity conflicts. The transference process (attributing to therapists or group members some aspects of relationships with significant others from their past) may result in rejection of the authority of an adult therapist in individual therapy. However, in the group this process is diluted by positive identification with group members.

By modeling therapists' functioning, group members learn to explore underlying feelings and to develop interpretations of the group behavior and verbal material. This presumably leads to insights into unconscious motivations and conflicts. The analyst or therapist helps the group accept interpretations, attempts to create a positive transference between therapist and group, and allows the group to "try out" a range of psychosocial behaviors and reactions focused on sharing and working through problems of their identity.

In their description of the general process of most therapeutic approaches, Chess and Hassibi (1978) list the following elements: (a) delineating problems, (b) examining maladaptive patterns through observations and verbal interaction, (c) confronting, clarifying, and interpreting, (d) gaining insight in a situationally relevant manner, and (e) presenting alternative strategies of interaction. Various therapeutic approaches differ as to the degree of emphasis on each element. Identity group psychotherapy focuses on clarification, interpretation, and insight. Other group approaches tend to focus on examination of maladaptive patterns and alternative strategies of interaction.

SOCIAL SKILLS DEVELOPMENT
AND OTHER SPECIALIZED GROUPS

STRUCTURED SOCIAL SKILLS
DEVELOPMENT GROUPS AND ACTIVITIES

In contrast to psychoanalytically oriented groups, which require a fairly high level of verbal functioning and cognitive organization for development of insight, social skills development groups may be quite concrete and focused on training in specific behaviors, such as anger control (Feindler & Ecton, 1988). Other social skills programs may address a wider range of behaviors and social functioning, but most typically employ some didactic training, modeling, rehearsal, reinforcement, and feedback (Wilkinson & Canter, 1982).

We have developed a number of structured adolescent group approaches, including a focused social skills development group program (Corder et al., 1979). Our approaches were developed with a population of adolescents who were shown to be fairly unsocialized, lacking in impulse control, and demonstrating chaotic life environments with limited opportunities for appropriate social learning or access to psychotherapeutic intervention (Naylor & Corder, 1976). Utilized in both outpatient and hospital settings, the program goals were to (a) provide reeducative social learning experiences, (b) reinforce acceptable behaviors with a behavior modification "point" system, (c) provide training in verbalization of feelings in an acceptable manner, (d) provide training and opportunities for peer feedback about behavior, and (e) arrange practice opportunities for the development of appropriate peer relationships and interactions.

Many of the activities used in the groups were in the form of therapeutic "games." For example, a "Successful and Unsuccessful Behavior Game" involves drill and didactic discussion of each basic step involved in communicating and in solving daily social interaction problems. Group members take turns pulling cards from a deck. The cards describe a number of simple interaction problems that require good communication, adequate presentation of the parameters of the problem, and the ability to suggest a compromise or offer inducements to others for their help. The group members take turns role-playing in both a successful and an unsuccessful scenario, which is preceded and followed by additional drills in the basic steps for problem solving. After each scenario the group members discuss the ability of the role-players to follow the basic steps of good problem solving.

An "Etiquette Olympics Game" involves videotaped demonstrations of a series of adequate social behaviors in a number of settings (e.g., table manners, introductions, etc.). After the behaviors required by the situation are broken down into manageable steps and discussed, members take turns role-playing these behaviors. The group members "score" their handling of the task by holding up large cards marked 1 through 10 to give their

"Olympic score" for the situation. Scores lower than 5 require repetition and drill.

The "Picking a Partner Game" focuses on helping members to (a) define friendship, (b) identify the factors that constitute a relationship between two people, and (c) practice approaching others using techniques for developing positive interactions which can develop into friendship. This game involves analyzing videotaped scenes using an original board game, and role-playing and discussing basic interaction skills. Topics include such questions as: How can you tell if someone is looking for a friend, or whether a group will let you become part of a conversation or other activity? What kind of eye contact and body language do people show to let you know whether you can approach them? How do you begin a conversation with a stranger? At times the group may use videotapes of their role-playing sessions to guide feedback discussions.

The "Family Script Game" requires each participant to develop a booklet which contains pages to identify the family member who "gets into the most trouble," "has difficulty getting what he or she wants," and so on. Participants also must identify the behaviors that result in these difficulties for family members. The booklet requires members to identify behaviors of their own that follow the "family script" and represent "unsuccessful problem solving." Topics which surface are the subject of further exercises.

The preceding games or exercises illustrate the strategies we use to involve participants in treatment. These techniques appear to offer positive opportunities for interesting and non-threatening peer interactions and development of basic social communication skills. We have found them effective with adolescents with limited verbal and cognitive organizational skills.

ECLECTIC STRUCTURED GROUPS
WITH LIMITED INSIGHT GOALS

Chapter 9 reviews in detail our structured adolescent group approach. In time-limited groups which combine both specific skills development training and limited insight goals, we have observed a need for techniques that structure group interaction to insure optimum participation and opportunities for peer feedback. This feedback is aimed at developing insight into behavior patterns. In addition, it provides a focus for teaching and modeling specific "mastery behaviors" for effective problem solving. The methods used in this type of approach with adolescent groups include (a) random assignment of group "roles" (e.g., rules enforcer, summarizer, positive stroker, protector, etc.) or responsibility for group functions, (b) use of therapeutic games to practice problem solving, and (c) development of individual "goal books" which outline behaviors and life pattern changes the adolescent would like to attempt. Specific exercises and homework are recorded in the goal book, as well as "peer grading" on the progress toward these goals. Other multimodal techniques used in the groups are negotiation and positive assertive exercises, biofeedback and relaxation exercises, self-concept improvement exercises, and group interactions with parents in a "parent hot seat" format.

COMPARISONS: ADVANTAGES AND DISADVANTAGES OF VARIOUS GROUP APPROACHES

Table 1 (p. 6) describes three types of groups commonly used for work with adolescents. Each type of group may be helpful to a particular type of client, depending on the treatment goals. Also, with each type of group there are advantages and limitations that the therapist must consider.

It appears possible that, given high levels of verbal skills, cognitive functioning, and motivational levels along with resources for long-term treatment, insight-oriented group approaches that emphasize interpretation and personality reorganization may be a treatment of choice. At the other end of the continuum, when fairly short-term treatment is necessary for adolescents with limited verbal, social, and cognitive skills, a highly specific and structured approach to identified problem areas, similar to the social skills groups described previously, should probably be considered. The structured group with limited insight goals described in Chapter 9 falls into the middle range of requirements for participation and functioning. Without the luxury of unlimited time for a "natural" development of group roles and functions, the assignment of group roles and functions usually facilitates the treatment experience and encourages feedback.

CURATIVE FACTORS IN ADOLESCENT GROUPS

Regardless of the therapist's theoretical approach, some basic concepts seem relevant to any group work with adolescents.

TABLE 1: ADOLESCENT GROUP STRUCTURE AND GOALS

STRUCTURE	LOW ──────────────────────► HIGH		
Type	• Psychoanalytically Oriented Identity Group Therapy	• Eclectic Structured Groups	• Social Skills Development Groups
Focus	• Insight • Positive Peer Identification	• Limited Insight • Improved Role Functioning • Improved Problem-Solving Skills	• Development of Specific Behavior Skills • Improved Problem-Solving Skills
Best Client	• Motivated • Higher Level Verbal and Cognitive Skills	• Either Type Depending on Treatment Goals	• Identified Problem • Limited Verbal, Cognitive, Social Skills
Time Frame	• Longer Term	• Time-Limited	• Set Number of Sessions
Sample Tasks	• Use of Transference • Interpretation • Therapist Modeling • "Try Out" New Behaviors	• Peer Feedback Aimed at Limited Insight • Assigning Roles and Responsibilities • Problem-Solving Practice • Goal Setting	• Didactic Training Modeling • Behavior Rehearsal • Reinforcement • Structured Feedback Exercises

Aside from the therapist's evaluation of the efficacy of group intervention techniques, the adolescent patients themselves must perceive the group process as helpful if they are to make a commitment to the group. Even within many residential settings, group treatment is not forced on resistant patients after initial trials, although they may have to forego certain privileges if they choose to refuse a particular treatment modality.

In previous research with my co-workers (Corder, Whiteside, & Haizlip, 1980), we investigated the group conditions and experiences that adolescents perceive as promoting positive changes. Research by Yalom (1970) has led to the description of a list of mechanisms and conditions in groups, labeled *curative factors*, which are perceived as promoting positive behavior change. These categories of conditions and group processes have been described as altruism, group cohesiveness, universality, guidance, identification, catharsis, insight, interpersonal learning (input and output), family reenactment, and existential awareness. Prior research had concentrated on adult groups, and, because adolescent psychotherapy goals and techniques differ appreciably from some facets of adult psychotherapy (Corder, Whiteside, & Vogel, 1977; Sugar, 1975), our own research examined differences between adolescent and adult perceptions of curative factors in group psychotherapy.

We examined adolescent group participants in four different treatment settings. They were participants in groups that averaged 9 months to 1 year in duration. Goals of the groups generally involved (a) working toward a better integrated locus of control over behavior through development of insight into group members' actions and behaviors and (b) offering opportunities for social learning and interaction with peers.

Using a card-sorting task, the adolescent patients were asked to describe the helpfulness of the curative factors described by Yalom. Subsequent interviews were used to confirm the results. Table 2 (p. 8) describes the factors selected as "most helpful" or "extremely helpful" by at least 25% of the subjects.

Table 3 (p. 9) shows factors ranked as least helpful by adolescents, and includes all items chosen by 25% or more of the subjects in the "less helpful" and "least helpful" categories.

We found that adolescents show patterns of perception that are similar to adults, with a few notable differences. Four of the same items or curative factors listed as most helpful by adolescents were the same as the five items ranked highest by adults (from the catharsis, interpersonal learning, and existential

**TABLE 2: FACTORS SELECTED AS MOST HELPFUL
BY ADOLESCENTS**

CATEGORY	PERCENT SELECTING	DESCRIPTION OF FACTOR
Catharsis	44%	Being able to say what was bothering me instead of holding it in.
Catharsis	38%	Learning how to express my feelings.
Existential	38%	Learning that I must take ultimate responsibility for the way I live my life, no matter how much guidance and support I get from others.
Interpersonal Learning (Input)	38%	Other members honestly telling me what they think of me.
Family Reenactment	31%	Being in the group was, in a sense, like being in a big family, only this time, a more accepting and understanding family.
Group Cohesiveness	25%	Belonging to a group of people who understood and accepted me.
Interpersonal Learning (Output)	25%	The group's giving me an opportunity to learn to approach others.
Universality	25%	Seeing I was as well off as others.
Altruism	25%	Helping others and being important in their lives.

factors categories). Differences were noted in the adults' higher ranking of items from the insight category, such as, "Discover-

TABLE 3: FACTORS SELECTED AS LEAST HELPFUL
BY ADOLESCENTS

CATEGORY	PERCENT SELECTING	DESCRIPTION OF FACTOR
Insight	60%	Learning I react to some people or situations unrealistically with feelings that somehow belong to earlier periods of my life.
Catharsis	40%	Expressing negative and/or positive feelings toward the group leader.
Identification	33%	Finding someone in the group I could pattern myself after.
Interpersonal Learning (Input)	27%	Learning that sometimes I confuse people by not saying what I really think.
Guidance	27%	Group members telling me what to do.
Identification	27%	Trying to be like someone in the group who was better adjusted than I.
Insight	27%	Learning that how I feel and behave today is related to my childhood and development.
Existential Factors	27%	Recognizing that, no matter how close I get to other people, I must still face life alone.

ing and accepting previously unknown and unacceptable parts of myself."

The adolescent groups tended to give the highest rankings to items describing the importance of group cohesiveness and feelings of universality, as well as those emphasizing the importance of interrelationships among group members. This finding appears to support the concepts of R. Shapiro et al. (1975), who emphasized the relationship between adolescent tasks in identity formation and the opportunities for exploration and development of self-perception which take place in the communication of self-perception among group members.

In using these results as a guide in setting goals and choosing techniques for adolescent groups, it may be helpful to review some typical statements from literature describing objectives for adolescent groups. Berkowitz and Sugar (1975) list the following goals and purposes for adolescent group membership:

1. To support assistance and confrontation from peers.
2. To provide a miniature real life situation.
3. To stimulate new ways of dealing with situations and developing new skills in human relations.
4. To stimulate new concepts of self and new models of identification.
5. To feel less isolated.
6. To provide a feeling of protection from the adult world while undergoing changes.
7. To help maintain continued self-examination as a bind to therapy.
8. To allow the swings of rebellion or submission that encourage independence and identification with the leader.
9. To uncover relationship problems not evident in individual therapy.

Our research shows that adolescents tend to value most highly the experiences described in goals 1, 3, and 5 above. The importance which the subjects placed on opportunities for interpersonal feedback (both input and output) suggests that techniques which insure increased opportunities for peer feedback and expression of feelings may heighten the adolescent's positive perception of the group.

The structured adolescent group approach emphasized in this book is aimed at optimizing the opportunities for the curative factors to develop from and through the group process.

REFERENCES

Berkowitz, I., & Sugar, M. (1975). Indications and contraindications for adolescent group psychotherapy. In M. Sugar

(Ed.), *The Adolescent in Group and Family Therapy* (pp. 3-26). New York: Brunner/Mazel.

Chess, S., & Hassibi, M. (1978). *Principles and Practice of Child Psychiatry*. New York: Plenum.

Corder, B. F., Whiteside, R., & Haizlip, T. (1980). A study of curative factors in group psychotherapy with adolescents. *International Journal of Group Psychotherapy, 31,* 341-354.

Corder, B. F., Whiteside, R., Thorton, W., & Wall, S. (1979). Structured social skills learning activities utilized by inexperienced therapists to supplement adolescent therapy groups. *North Carolina Journal of Mental Health, 10,* 19-23.

Corder, B. F., Whiteside, R., & Vogel, M. (1977). A therapeutic game for structuring and facilitating group psychotherapy with adolescents. *Adolescence, 47,* 261-286.

Feindler, E., & Ecton, R. (1988). *Adolescent Anger Control*. New York: Pergamon.

Naylor, K., & Corder, B. F. (1976). Evaluation of adolescent treatment needs and assessment of service deficiencies in treatment and follow-up of hospitalized adolescents. *North Carolina Journal of Mental Health, 4,* 51-62.

Rachman, A. (1975). *Identity Group Psychotherapy with Adolescents*. Springfield, IL: Charles C. Thomas.

Shapiro, R., Zinner, J., Berkowitz, D., & Shapiro, E. (1975). The impact of group experiences on adolescent development. In M. Sugar (Ed.), *The Adolescent in Group and Family Therapy* (pp. 69- 86). New York: Brunner/Mazel.

Sugar, M. (Ed.). (1975). *The Adolescent in Group and Family Therapy*. New York: Brunner/Mazel.

Wilkinson, J., & Canter, S. (1982). *A Social Skills Training Manual*. New York: John Wiley & Sons.

Yalom, E. (1970). *The Theory and Practice of Group Psychotherapy*. New York: Basic Books.

2

THERAPISTS' ROLES
AND FUNCTIONS IN
ADOLESCENT GROUPS

The differences in functioning by therapists in adult and adolescent groups have been summarized by Sugar (1975), MacLennan and Felsenfeld (1968), Masterson (1968), and others. These differences in group process and therapists' techniques have included (a) higher levels of anxiety and difficulty in dealing with direct interpretation for behavior in adolescent groups, (b) the necessity for focus on the specific tasks of adolescence in their groups (e.g., separation family, clarification of sex roles, etc.) which ideally have been mastered, at least to some degree, by adult group members, (c) lower expectations for self-analysis by adolescents, (d) typical adolescent focus on conflicts with authority figures, and (e) adolescents' greater tendency to utilize activity and acting-out behaviors to handle anxiety generated within the group.

In some of our previous research, my associates and I have attempted to isolate therapists' behaviors that tend to be specific to their work with adolescents (Corder, Haizlip, & Walker, 1980). Our findings indicate that experienced (10 or more years) group therapists generally described their functioning in adolescent groups as showing more verbal activity, more openness in describing personal experiences, and lower expectations for any member self-analysis or group-initiated attempts to structure the group process. Experienced therapists felt their verbal output was more direct, frequent, and characterized by a focus on *clarification* of members' verbalizations, rather than on analysis of the content. They also felt they took more responsibility for modeling verbal input and acceptance of feedback in adolescent groups. Adolescent group process was also described as more rapid because of the higher levels of verbal and physical activity. In addition, they described adolescent groups as tending to be shorter in duration and ending more abruptly than adult groups. These therapists also viewed the "group mix" of members in adolescent groups as a more significant issue because of the rapid group process and comparatively lower skill levels for dealing with stress and anxiety.

Inexperienced therapists generally perceived adolescents as less motivated, because they were not usually self-referred to groups. Specific difficulties in providing feedback to parents and agencies were noted, along with increased difficulty over confidentiality issues and ambivalence toward authority figures. The inexperienced therapists also felt that the adolescent group's limited social skill and ability to deal with anxiety required additional selection criteria for adolescent group membership. Difficulty with establishing effective treatment contracts and a focus on developmentally related themes in adolescent groups were noted.

The headings that follow represent questions addressed by the research of the author and her colleagues comparing experienced and inexperienced therapists. Our purpose in discussing these differences is to encourage readers to examine their own styles when working with adolescent groups.

QUESTIONS

In what specific behaviors do you see your role as a therapist differ between adolescent and adult groups?

Experienced therapists described their increased verbal output and tendency to limit periods of silence in adolescent groups. They described themselves as being more directive, doing more clarifying of group verbal output, and allowing more opportunities for modeling of problem solving in adolescent groups. In addition, their expectations for self-analysis by members were lower. In general, they felt they were more confronting in adolescent groups in order to deal with adolescents' tendency to use denial.

Inexperienced therapists described themselves as more verbally active and as using more clarifying statements in adolescent groups. However, they also focused on the increased amount of therapist's time required for limit-setting and handling high activity levels in adolescent groups. In contrast with the more experienced group, they perceived themselves as *less* confronting in adolescent groups. They tended to emphasize the importance of their function as a role model for problem solving and socially acceptable behavior for the adolescent groups.

Do you use any specific structured therapy techniques more regularly with adolescents?

Less experienced therapists verbalized a higher need for structuring therapy sessions with adolescents, but were able to describe only a limited number of techniques to provide this structure. They tended to rely primarily on role-play or modified psychodrama techniques.

Experienced therapists also perceived adolescent groups as requiring more structure than adult groups, and often used role-play or modified psychodrama techniques. However, they appeared to have a much wider range of methods for insuring adequate participation and input in the adolescent groups. Several therapists mentioned a number of warm-up exercises which they used in initial sessions, and described a few therapeutic games they found useful in sessions. Chapter 9 includes descriptions of structured exercises the author and her colleagues have found effective.

Are there any unique aspects of establishing therapeutic contracts with adolescents in group psychotherapy?

Both groups of therapists agreed that establishing a therapeutic contract with adolescents was more difficult because of conflicts over authority issues, concerns about confidentiality, and the necessity for feedback to parents, schools, and so forth. Experienced therapists tended to plan for initial individual sessions to strengthen the understanding of and agreement to the contract. They were quite explicit and detailed in outlining their expectations for therapy goals, limitations on absences, requirements for group participation, individual goal setting by adolescents, and so on. Some therapists required a written therapy contract to be signed by parents and adolescents which presented a formal description of goals, limits, and expectations, along with the individual therapy goals selected by the adolescent.

What are the most frequent problem areas for
you as a therapist in dealing with adolescent
groups? Were these different from adult groups?

All inexperienced therapists listed concerns over handling verbal and physical aggression, as well as primitive verbalizations involving sexuality, in adolescent groups. They described handling these situations in a more restrictive fashion than in adult groups. They summarized their actions as tending to be "more authoritarian," using more limit–setting and involving more instances of temporary exclusion from the group.

By contrast, the experienced therapists listed no specific concerns over handling aggression or sexuality in either adolescent or adult groups. Their concerns centered around the difficulties of mixing adolescents who were functioning at widely different intellectual and social levels in a single group. Several stated that the adolescent groups tended to be pulled down to the functional levels of the lowest functioning members.

Do you use specifically different guidelines
for selection of members for adult and adolescent
groups? Are there any specific diagnostic and
problem categories for which you think group
treatment is contraindicated for adolescents?

Inexperienced therapists stated that they established more stringent guidelines for membership in adolescent groups than in adult ones. Most reported that they might exclude adolescent patients who were diagnosed as psychotic or mentally retarded, or who showed severe physical handicaps, severe acting out, and/or substance addictions. In general they tended to deal with a very limited age range of members.

Experienced therapists did not exclude specific diagnostic categories from adult or adolescent groups, except for listing acute psychosis as a contraindication for referral. Generally, they focused on the importance of the "group mix" in a specific group, describing a need for a balance between withdrawn, acting out, and verbally passive or verbally active group participants. These therapists felt that the inclusion of any patient who was severely deviant from the others (in level of intellectual or social functioning) tended to slow group process. It also required more intervention by the therapist to avoid scapegoating of the deviant member. Some therapists reported using diagnostic screening groups as an initial referral point for adolescents to assess their functioning before referring them to ongoing treatment groups.

How is assessment of progress and
feedback of information about progress
handled differently in adolescent groups?

In contrast with inexperienced therapists, the experienced group tended to have more continuing contact with parents and schools for feedback about adolescents in their groups. Inexperienced therapists either placed less emphasis on feedback, or had not developed specific feedback mechanisms.

All therapists utilized subjective reports by adults and adolescent group members as measures of progress, but experienced therapists tended to require additional outside feedback as evaluation measures, along with some structured evaluation forms.

What behaviors do you consciously
model for adolescent and adult groups?

Both therapist groups felt that adult groups had less need for modeling of positive behaviors. Therapists reported modeling expression of feelings, acceptance of others, and methods of giving and receiving feedback about behavior in adolescent groups.

What important areas of therapists'
functioning would you emphasize in a training
program for group psychotherapy with adolescents?

Both therapists' groups described the necessity for learning about developmental phases and developmental tasks present in normal adolescence. Experienced therapists noted that the adolescent group therapists should have coped fairly adequately with their *own* adolescent developmental tasks, and have a clear knowledge about their difficulties in these areas. The experienced therapists noted the need for adolescent group therapists to have a greater ability to handle high anxiety levels and more group dysfunction.

Inexperienced therapists perceived a higher need for programs that could teach specific techniques for structuring adolescent groups and for handling any incidents of physical aggression or inappropriate expressions of sexuality. They also noted a preference for male and female co-therapy relationships, particularly in adolescent groups, to provide opportunities for modeling appropriate social behaviors.

CHOOSING AND WORKING WITH A CO-THERAPIST IN ADOLESCENT GROUPS

It is widely reported that having male and female co-therapists in adolescent groups offers opportunities for role modeling for both sexes (Skynner, 1976). In addition, co-therapy provides a forum for modeling shared problem solving, alternative leadership during the absence of one therapist, and a mutual support system for the therapists when group process becomes difficult or frustrating (Dick, Lessler, & Whiteside, 1980). However, it also adds another dimension to the already complex personal relationship between two therapists, who may have struggles with dominance, differing theoretical orientations, and perceived "ownership" of the group. Developing a nonsexist, shared orientation toward group leadership and problem solving may be one of the most critical factors in planning for any group.

Given the potential for selecting from a pool of therapists, how should you begin selecting a co-therapist? Earlier reviews of literature related to co-therapy relationships seldom focused on factors that might be helpful in an initial prediction of success in the co-therapy relationship (Paulson, Burroughs, & Gelb, 1976). This same study (Paulson et al., 1976) reported responses by co-therapists to questionnaires on factors related to agreement and disagreement between them and to their general satisfaction with the relationship. Conflicts appeared to be centered around (a) differences in approaches to solving problems within the group, (b) differences in perception of acceptable activity levels by the therapists, and (c) problems described as "differences in style and skill."

In a 1978 paper, Corder and Cornwall began a series of studies aimed at developing nonthreatening techniques for helping co-therapists identify potential problem areas in functioning. Goals included correctly identifying their own and their co-therapists' group leadership patterns, and developing structured techniques for an effective, positive interchange in collaborative sessions.

THE METHOD USED IN THE STUDY

To begin the process, my co-therapist and I developed a list of categories that described behaviors and personality patterns which appeared critical to therapist functioning in groups. These categories were dominance, competitiveness, supportive-nurturance, critical-confronting, emphasis on cognitive functioning, emphasis on emotional functioning, passivity-activeness, flexibility-rigidity, openness-masking, and comfort in sex role.

We next asked therapists who were relative strangers to review treatment plan goals and theoretical orientation, followed by ratings of each other, and 12 weeks of co-leading groups. We then examined perceived differences between themselves and each other.

RESULTS AND DISCUSSION OF THE STUDY

An unusually high correlation was found between the frequency of categories noted as problem areas in collaborative sessions, and the categories in which there were three or more points difference between self-perception rankings and rankings of each other by the co-therapists. For example, co-therapists who showed a high frequency of disagreement during collaborative sessions around the amount of supportive focus needed for one of the group members were also likely to show the greatest differences between their perception of their own functioning and their co-therapist's perception of them. These pilot results suggested the importance of co-therapists clarifying their different orientations and communicating about different experiences in their groups.

In later research, Corder, Cornwall, and Whiteside (1984) extended their work on co-therapy functioning in adolescent therapy groups and developed a therapist rating scale from an expansion of the pilot study described above. A copy of this scale is shown on page 21.

In this same study, the authors developed a structured framework for initial planning and structure of co-therapy functioning in adolescent groups. They felt that agreement and discussion of these issues, which cover a wide range of group process and function, would provide a mutually satisfactory structure for group work and collaborative sessions. Therapists were first asked to answer a questionnaire *separately* (to identify differences in style and theory in a nonthreatening manner), and then to review each item with their co-therapist, reaching a compromise or mutually satisfactory solution. The structured questionnaire framework is shown on pages 22 to 27. Co-therapists may wish to use this questionnaire to guide their own planning and feedback sessions in practice. Throughout this book, the author's approach to these questions will be discussed under appropriate chapter headings.

THE COLLABORATIVE SESSION

Following each group session, therapists typically meet to review the group process, progress, and any potential problem areas. Corder et al. (1984) have utilized a "checklist" of curative factors in adolescent groups, supplemented by lists of individual members' various goals, as a standard for measuring the amount of significant group progress and "on-target" behaviors. Videotapes and/or therapists' weekly process notes are used to check the frequency of occurrence of behaviors perceived as examples of the curative factors described earlier. For individual group members, checks on frequency of verbal input and group behaviors related to their stated goals may also be helpful. These measures provide a more objective analysis of the effectiveness of current group functioning. A sample checklist is shown on pages 28 to 30 with sample comments included. This checklist may also include spaces for noting specific difficulties or problem areas in the group session.

THERAPIST RATING SCALE

Instructions: Although you may have limited social contact prior to working together as co-therapists, most leaders have some expectations and predictions about each other's behavior as a group leader following initial group planning meetings and contacts.

In this scale, you are being asked to rate yourself and your co-therapist on a scale of 1 to 10 (1 = lowest amount and 10 = highest amount) on each of the selected personality and behavioral characteristics, *as you would predict that they would be shown in group therapy sessions.*

CHARACTERISTIC	RATE YOURSELF	RATE YOUR CO-THERAPIST
Active		
Passive		
Flexible		
Rigid		
Dominant		
Submissive		
Cue Emitting (shows emotion in expression, etc.)		
Cue Suppressing		
Confronting		
Supportive		
Authoritarian		
Collegial (takes "equal partner" role)		
Nurturing		
Critical		
Cognitively, Intellectually Oriented		
Affectively Oriented		

PROBLEM AREAS AND
CRITICAL ISSUES IN GROUPS

Instructions: Please answer the following questions as fully as possible, since your answers will help to provide a framework for subsequent collaborative discussions.

1. What do you feel are the most important basic goals for any adolescent group? List at least five in order of your perception of their importance.

2. How do you feel the adolescent group members should be involved in formulating goals for the group?

3. How do you feel group rules should be established and enforced in the group?

4. Describe, in general terms, how much structure and therapists' input you feel is most productive for an adolescent group?

5. How would you measure progress toward goals in an adolescent group?

6. How important do you perceive the role of therapists' analytically oriented interpretation of group members' behavior to be? How much interpretation would you probably attempt in this adolescent group?

7. Describe your ideas about the importance of role-playing in adolescent groups. How and when would you use this technique? How would you introduce it initially and what role would you see each therapist taking in the process?

8. How do you believe feedback to staff and parents should be handled?

9. Describe confidentiality measures you would like to have for information and records.

10. How important do you feel the process of modeling acceptable adult behavior (by the therapist) is to the adolescent group therapy process? What types of behavior do you plan to model?

11. How do you assess the level of anxiety in a group? How do you describe nonproductive anxiety levels in an adolescent group? What would you do to rectify this?

12. Describe your approach to selection of members and pre-therapy training of members.

13. What techniques do you use to begin and end adolescent group sessions?

14. What types of recordkeeping would you like to use for these sessions?

15. How do you wish to introduce new members and terminate old members in an ongoing adolescent group?

16. What are some of the techniques (relaxation, pairing, etc.) that you like to use in structuring and facilitating adolescent groups?

17. How do you feel co-therapists can "even up" their input into an adolescent group? How do you feel this partnership should be balanced, and what are your ideas for you and your co-therapist?

18. Describe how much openness between co-therapists you feel is most effective in adolescent groups.

19. Would you handle some types of conflicts between you and your co-therapist openly in the group session? Give reasons and examples.

20. Describe your ideas about how weekly collaborative sessions for you and your co-therapist could be handled that would be most helpful to you. What information, feedback, and methods of review do you find helpful?

Instructions: For the following questions, please give *two separate answers for each question.* Answer (a) as you would handle the problem if you were the single therapist in an adolescent group and (b) as you would like to see the problem handled by co-therapists leading an adolescent group.

21. Under what circumstances would you interrupt an extended silence in the group and how would you handle this situation?

    a.

    b.

22. Under what circumstances would you strongly confront a group member about the content of their verbal material and how would you do this?

    a.

    b.

23. How would you handle a group member who verbally monopolized sessions?

    a.

    b.

24. How would you handle a group member's being scapegoated?

    a.

    b.

25. How would you handle a group member's becoming physically aggressive in group?

    a.

    b.

26. How would you handle a group member who is withdrawn and did not speak for almost a whole group session?

    a.

    b.

27. How do you handle a group member suddenly becoming upset and dashing from the room?

    a.

    b.

28. How would you respond to a group member suddenly exhibiting bizarre, psychotic behavior in the group?

    a.

    b.

29. How would you handle sexual acting out between group members that is reported within the group?

    a.

    b.

30. How would you deal with sexually explicit material brought out in the group?

    a.

    b.

31. Do you feel the male to female ratio of adolescent group members is critical? How would you structure this if membership changed radically during an ongoing group?

    a.

    b.

32. How would you deal with complaints and highly negative statements made in the group toward other staff?

    a.

    b.

33. How would you recognize and deal with a member's sharing excessively intimate material too early in the group process (e.g., relating incest experiences in the first group session)?

    a.

    b.

34. If some group members are involved in other types of therapy, how do you feel group experiences can be integrated? Are there some issues you feel should be handled only in individual therapy sessions?

    a.

    b.

COLLABORATIVE SESSION
CHECKLIST OF GROUP PROCESS

DATE_____   SESSION NO._____   GROUP_____

CURATIVE FACTORS	DESCRIPTION OF RELATED GROUP INPUT/BEHAVIOR
Saying what was bothering me.	A.M. - discussed reasons for refusing medica-tions; G.L. - discussed concerns about home visit.
Learning how to express feelings	A.M. - practiced how to verbalize to aides, re: medication; G.L. - encouraged to discuss home visit with parents on phone.
Taking responsibility for my own actions	G.M. - confronted by group on complaints about staff mistreatment, re: behaviors which lead to restrictions. G.M. - seemed to accept some responsibility.
Interpersonal Learning/Input	Group confrontation of G.M.
Family Reenactment	No example.
Group Cohesiveness	Group asked to plan an activity together outside the group.
Interpersonal Learning/Output	Role-play in helping G.M. perceive and discuss his ways of communicating needs to staff (G.M., G.L., R.C.).

CURATIVE FACTORS	DESCRIPTION OF RELATED GROUP INPUT/BEHAVIOR
Universality	No specific example verbalized.
Altruism	Group given "positive strokes" by leaders for their assistance to G.M.

OTHER ASPECTS OF SESSION

Describe any perceived difficulties in handling group process:

1. **Between You and Co-Therapist**: B.C. introduced role-play without consulting R.W., who felt the group might have initiated this process if therapists had delayed their input slightly.
2. **Among Group Members**: G.M. may need help limiting his time for verbalization to allow others to make input.

Any issues or topics which were "unfinished business" and should be continued in next weekly session:

Some feedback from staff indicates that R.C. may also at times demonstrate some of the same lack of effective communication discussed for G.M. Perhaps more role-play needed on "successful and unsuccessful behavior."

List members who participated minimally in group and who should be encouraged in next session:

W.S. attentive and alert, but made little or no verbal input into the group; possibly group therapeutic game needs to be used to force his participation in nonthreatening way.

INDIVIDUAL GOALS FOR MEMBERS -
NOTES ON THEIR PROGRESS

NAME	GOAL	NOTE ON PROCESS AND PROGRESS
G.M.	"Getting along with others"	Responded well to role-play (e.g., communication with staff). Showed ability to change verbal behavior in role-play.
A.L.	"Moving away from parents to be more inde- pendent."	Able to make some small steps; applied for drivers' course.

REFERENCES

Corder, B. F., & Cornwall, T. (1978). A pilot study approach to prediction of problem areas in male-female cotherapy relationships. *North Carolina Journal of Mental Health, 8,* 35-36.

Corder, B. F., Cornwall, T., & Whiteside, R. (1984). Techniques for increasing effectiveness of cotherapy functions in adolescent psychotherapy groups. *International Journal of Group Psychotherapy, 34,* 643-654.

Corder, B. F., Haizlip, T., & Walker, P. (1980). Critical areas of therapists' functioning in adolescent group psychotherapy: A comparison with self-perception of functioning in adult groups. *Adolescence, 58,* 435-442.

Dick, R., Lessler, K., & Whiteside, R. (1980). A developmental framework for cotherapy. *International Journal of Group Psychotherapy, 3,* 273-283.

MacLennan, B., & Felsenfeld, N. (1968). *Group Counseling and Psychotherapy with Adolescents.* New York: Columbia University Press.

Masterson, J. F. (1968). Psychotherapy of adolescents contrasted with psychotherapy of adults. *Journal of Nervous and Mental Diseases, 127,* 517-551.

Paulson, I., Burroughs, J., & Gelb, C. (1976). Cotherapy: What is the crux of the relationship? *International Journal of Group Psychotherapy, 26,* 213-224.

Skynner, A. (1976). *Systems of Family and Marital Psychotherapy.* New York: Brunner/Mazel.

Sugar, M. (Ed). (1975). *The Adolescent in Group and Family Therapy.* New York: Brunner/Mazel.

3

ADMINISTRATIVE AND LEGAL ISSUES IN FORMING ADOLESCENT GROUPS

Whether preparing for a group or a garden, the planning for the project may be the most crucial factor in deciding the quality of the eventual product. In any facility setting, it is first necessary to establish the "ownership" of the group and the parameters of the therapist's autonomy for decision making about the group. In a private practice setting, planning for handling feedback to parents, clients, and schools must be considered along with a wide range of other administrative issues.

THE FACILITY OR INPATIENT SETTING

The location of the therapy group within the administrative flow chart of the facility must be established in a concrete fashion. Within established lines of administration, who is directly responsible for decision making about the group? Under which procedure manual are the activities of the therapy group covered? These are important issues in the day-to-day functioning of the group and in legal considerations that may affect insurance coverage, responsibility, and liability for the group and its activities. If there are no adequate procedure manuals which cover the functioning of the groups, establishing these guidelines may be the therapist's first priority.

GROUP THERAPY AS A PRIMARY
OR ADJUNCT THERAPY PROCESS

Therapists should consider the following critical questions. Will the group function as the primary treatment modality for clients? Will the group therapist also have to function as the case administrator for group members? If individual therapy is considered the primary mode of treatment, how will collaboration, feedback, and treatment planning be organized with the staff member who is considered the primary therapist? There are a number of issues and questions which will have to be addressed in this situation. Will the individual therapist consider group process to be "draining the energy from individual sessions"? Is there agreement on the focus of treatment goals? Will the group therapist have any input into the gain and loss of privileges? Will consistent participation in group therapy be established as a requirement for maintaining group members' unit privileges? Will the group members represent a mixture of treatment emphasis (group assigned as primary treatment for some members, and adjunct treatment for others)?

How and by whom will noncompliance and nonattendance be handled? In some facilities, patients are required to attend individual sessions; group attendance may be enforced by loss of privileges but may not be grounds for expulsion from the program on the basis of noncompliance with treatment. In many cases, it has been helpful to have separate case administrators for members of inpatient therapy groups.

SUPERVISION

Will there be regular supervision of your work in the group? If there is no supervision available, will you be free to seek supervision outside your facility staff? Will there be at least a responsible staff person with whom you may check out your perception of the function and process of your group therapy program on some regular basis?

Good supervision will increase a group therapist's skills, keep motivation levels high, and, when supervisory groups are available, offer peer feedback about group process and the therapist's interventions. Where no other experienced group therapists are available on a facility's staff, some contracting with other facilities for supervision may be an option.

Many therapists prefer to use videotapes of group sessions as the basis for their work with supervisors. Of course, adequate consent for videotaping for any purpose is necessary from responsible parents or guardians, and often from the adolescent group members themselves. Audiotapes should be used to supplement written notes on group process when videotapes are not available. Memory of the group process and the therapist's interventions and reactions is seldom completely accurate and unbiased.

To utilize supervision most effectively, therapists should formulate answers to the following questions to be shared with their supervisors: How do I seem to learn most adequately? Do I need visual feedback from videotapes or observations of others in groups? Do I learn effectively from role-playing various intervention techniques with my supervisor, or is this too anxiety provoking for me?   Considering limits on most supervisory time, is it typically more helpful for me to appear with a list of questions about the weekly session, or to review the process step by step from notes, videotapes, or audiotapes?

In my experience, unsatisfactory supervision experiences seem to be related to lack of mutual understanding of what both the supervisor and the trainee should receive and provide during the sessions. Do you want to have extensive "suggestions" for alternative behaviors and interventions provided by your supervisor? Do you prefer an exchange on issues you have selected for each session? If your supervisor also evaluates your other work performance, or is your immediate superior, will this affect your willingness to display any conflicts and unsuccessful interventions from the group sessions?

It may be helpful for some supervisors and trainees to use a record similar to the one on pages 41 to 42 for the most effective use of supervisory time.

CONFIDENTIALITY
AND RECORDKEEPING

How will your records for the group differ from individual therapy records? Some redistribution of administrative duties will be necessary if group therapists are expected to make separate notes in each group member's chart. One option may consist of having the therapist write a single summary of group process from each session to be included in each member's chart. Confidentiality for the individual records may be handled by identifying each patient by number or initials, and labeling each individual record copy with the specific patient's number or initial. Treatment facilities normally have procedure guidelines for confidentiality which outline methods for separating information about group interactions for inclusion in individual charts and records.

When a single weekly group report is adequate, it may be possible to use a structured format similar to that described in Chapter 7 ("Pre- and Post-Testing for Adolescent Groups"). In any case, the method of reporting on group process should be explained carefully and explicitly to all group members.

Clearly, some restrictions related to confidentiality do not normally apply to information indicating that a patient may be planning self-destructive behavior or behavior that could be injurious to others. Therapists should clarify in their own minds and for the group how confidentiality shall be defined.

OBSERVERS

Many facilities offer two-way mirror rooms for observation by trainees. Again, any legal constraints on the status of observers, or viewing of videotapes, should be checked with legal advisors in each facility. Because of adolescents' extreme sensitivity regarding confidentiality, observers typically represent a source of anxiety. Additional adults in the room may also discourage the growth of group cohesion.

THE PHYSICAL SETTING

Any room adequate for seating group members in a circular fashion should suffice for meetings. However, when working with adolescents, having all chairs exactly alike avoids conflicts over which member has the "leader chair," sofa, and so on. When working with extremely impulsive, aggressive adolescents, some therapists prefer a circular table surrounded by chairs for the initial group meetings. Others feel that any object as large as a conference table may interfere with group interactions. A small table for serving refreshments is helpful. Beanbag chairs and other pillowlike seating may cause some regression in adolescent group members, and the same concerns may apply to allowing members to sit on the floor during sessions. The benefits from the relaxed, informal atmosphere fostered by this type of seating should be balanced against the benefits of the "getting down to business" ambiance reflected in more formal, adult-oriented seating.

REFRESHMENTS

Many therapists feel that serving refreshments provides (a) a symbolic way of meeting dependency needs, (b) opportunities for negative comments to be directed toward the therapists/authority figures within the metaphor of complaints about and rejection of "inferior cookies," "cheap drinks," and so forth, (c) an activity that lowers anxiety levels by providing a nonthreatening, pleasurable group interaction, and (d) an opportunity for learning simple social skills and etiquette.

In my experience, refreshments should be simple (cookies or chips and soft drinks), and the responsibility for serving them politely and ceremoniously should be rotated among members. Setting a consistent time for serving the refreshments tends to cut down disruption of the group process. If the last 10 minutes are used for refreshments, the period can also be used to summarize the group themes and process (see Chapter 8). Alternatively, if they are served at the beginning of the group, the serving can become a part of settling down to work.

TIME FOR SESSIONS

One hour is a minimum time for a group of up to six members. For larger groups, at least 15 to 30 additional minutes are needed. My own experience has been that adolescents' attention span seldom lasts through sessions longer than 90 minutes.

There may be a few adolescents whose attention span is even more limited. On inpatient units it is possible to allow an adolescent to attend one-half of the group session until his or her behavior and impulse control improve enough to allow attendance through a complete session.

CLOSED VERSUS OPEN GROUPS -
TIME-LIMITED VERSUS CONTINUING GROUPS

Time-limited groups are often focused on a specific problem area (e.g., eating disorders, aggression control). The advantages of these groups include lowering initial resistance for referral by parents and members' increased acceptance of the necessity for setting focused, specific goals. Another obvious advantage is the increased capacity for treating larger numbers of clients in facility settings where there is pressure for delivery of services. Disadvantages of the time-limited group include limitations on the depth of treatment and intervention, and the reluctance of members to leave a group that they perceive as helpful, accepting, and supportive.

Open-ended, continuing groups tend to have several advantages. They (a) allow for addressing problem areas in depth, (b) provide a nucleus of experienced, effective group members who can model adequate participation behaviors for new members, and (c) allow for longer term commitment and affiliation by members.

The disadvantages are that (a) parents and sometimes group members themselves may feel there is not the same specific goal-oriented focus for long-term groups, (b) some insurance companies and health care plans cover only a limited number of sessions, and (c) fewer clients can be served.

Several combinations and alternative types of groups have been used by the author and co-workers. A time-limited group, focused on presenting problem areas and specific goal setting, may be the initial group to which all clients are referred. After attending this group, members may "graduate" when they meet specific behavioral goals outlined in their group contract, or they may choose to transfer to a second, ongoing, longer term group. Members of the second group list goals that include more intensive work on a wider range of personality and behavior issues. Another format has been to develop a structured, open ended group which allows some members to "graduate" after reaching limited goals, and allows others to continue in the group as "peer mentors." These peer mentors work on expanded, deeper issues of their own while helping new members learn effective group participation behaviors. The advantage of this approach is to allow some patients to feel a sense of accomplishment after meeting limited goals, while rewarding others by developing a further sense of mastery through helping others as they continue to deal with their own expanded goals.

LEGAL ISSUES

Legal standards for mental health services are constantly being reviewed in most states. This book is not capable of addressing specific statutes or comprehensively examining legal issues related to treatment of adolescent clients. The following information covers some basic tenets which should be considered in formulating any treatment approach.

Our own legal advisors have stated that, other than actions taken by a limited number of nonethical professionals or clients, litigation typically stems from misunderstandings regarding the goals, expectations, purposes, and techniques involved in therapy. Adequate written documentation of a mutually agreed-upon understanding of these goals and techniques, as well as continuing feedback to responsible parties, are seen as the basic tools for avoiding potential litigation. This has been one of the motivations for the development of the written therapy contract discussed in Chapter 5.

Our legal consultants have also suggested some of the following basic guidelines for treatment programs (Corder, Haizlip, & Spears, 1976):

1. Remember that service providers and facilities may have legal actions brought against them at any time. Any aspect of treatment and services is a potential source of litigation. The service provider can only take steps to insure that it will be difficult or impossible for a suit to be brought against their programs *successfully*.
2. Each facility or service provider should have available a legal consultant who can approve each consent form and make recommendations regarding the signatures, witnesses, and notarization required for each form.
3. Each aspect of the treatment program should be covered by a manual which clearly describes procedures, rules, and guidelines. The manual should be reviewed and approved by a legal consultant.
4. All aspects of the treatment program should be carefully explained to the adolescent and his or her parents. Some

    documentation of the mutual understanding of that explanation should be present in records.

5. Any aspect of treatment that might affect patient confidentiality should have special scrutiny. This would include use of videotapes, case histories used for educational purposes, photographs, newspaper releases, and so on. Specific forms for each of these required consents should be developed. All permission forms should describe in detail how the information will be used, in language explicit enough to allow an average person to understand. This helps to insure that a truly informed consent exists between service provider and client. It should be noted, however, that patients may rescind a permission or consent form at any time, and that time limits are usually required on any consent form.

    Some of the special areas of confidentiality involved in group work include recording group process in several patients' charts while protecting the privacy of individual patients, and providing feedback to parents and others on individual member's participation without compromising the privacy of other group members. Insuring confidentiality of group information among patients outside the group is a source of concern, as well as the necessity for requiring consent from *all* group members for videotaping or recording of sessions. Any limitations on confidentiality rules (reporting illegal or self-destructive actions, inability to rigidly enforce confidentiality rules outside the group) should be described, and mutual understanding by both parents and adolescents should be documented.

6. Treatment contracts are often helpful in documenting mutual expectations of therapists, patients, and parents in group work (see Chapter 5).

SUPERVISION AND SESSION RECORD

GROUP_____ DATE_____ THERAPIST_____

Major Themes in Group for this Session:

Theme   **Who Initiated Theme?**
                                             (member, therapist)

Therapist-Initiated Interventions (role-play, other exercises, confronta-tion, clarification, interpretation):

Intervention   **Problem?**

Examples of Curative Factors Operating in Adolescent Group:

Factor	Description of Group Input/Behavior
Saying what was bothering me	
Learning how to express feelings	
Taking responsibility for the way I live my life	
Interpersonal Learning/Input	
Family Reenactment	

*Examples of Curative Factors Operating in
Adolescent Group* (Continued):

Factor	Description of Group Input/Behavior
Group Cohesiveness	
Interpersonal Learning/Output	
Universality	
Altruism	

Perceived Problem Areas: *Suggested Alternatives:*

Therapist Interventions

*Suggested Focus or Emphasis for Next Session (interventions, specific
member focus, curative factor focus, unfinished business, etc.):*

REFERENCE

Corder, B. F., Haizlip, T., & Spears, L. (1976). Legal issues in the treatment of adolescent psychiatric inpatients. *Hospital and Community Psychiatry, 27,* 712-715.

4

MEMBER SELECTION AND GOAL SETTING

MEMBER SELECTION ISSUES: INDICATIONS AND CONTRAINDICATIONS FOR GROUP MEMBERSHIP

As noted in earlier chapters, more experienced group therapists tend to list a limited number of factors which they view as contraindications for group membership. In general the "group mix," or mixture of member characteristics within a particular group, appears to be a critical factor. As a clinical "rule of thumb," my experience in group selection supports the following recommendations: (a) It is helpful to include at least two members who are verbally active and likely to spontaneously provide verbal input into the group process. These members can balance the inclusion of two more withdrawn and passive members in that same group. (b) *More* than two passive, fairly nonverbal members in a six- to eight-member group tends to impede the group process severely. (c) More than two overly assertive, highly verbal members tends to overwhelm the less active participants. In general, when more structured techniques are used by leaders, a wider range of functioning within the group can still be handled effectively.

AGE ISSUES

Adolescents aged 13 to 17 are typically dealing with social and independence issues which are different from those younger, preadolescent youths. However, chronological age will often fail to differentiate social functioning levels. Many adolescents are "13 going on 31," while some 17-year-olds have not begun dating or dealing with other adolescent developmental tasks. An extremely immature teenager will present a tempting target for scapegoating by other members in adolescent groups. Protecting a member who is socially deviant from the response of other group members will constitute a time-consuming task for the therapists and often slows work on more critical issues for other group members.

MALE AND FEMALE ISSUES

Young adolescents under age 13 are often more comfortable in same-sex groups. At 13, they appear to appreciate the input and perceptions of opposite-sex members, and opportunities for practicing some social interactions with the opposite sex seem to be an attraction for many members. When possible, organize groups with an equal number of male and female members. This ideal group composition is not always feasible, and some adolescents have voiced discomfort when they became the sole male or female in a group. To avoid this, my co-workers and I normally assign at least two males to predominately female groups, and vice versa.

DIAGNOSTIC CRITERIA, GENERAL INDICATIONS, AND CONTRAINDICATIONS

In formulating selection criteria, diagnostic categories have not appeared to be as useful as the consideration of the present social functioning and verbal assertiveness level of an adolescent. The maintenance of a workable mixture and balance of group member characteristics, as described earlier, is the more critical issue.

Adolescents who are acutely psychotic should not be referred to most groups. The anxiety level of the group may become severe as the therapists are required to focus on the acute concerns and lack of reality contact shown by the acutely psychotic patient (hallucinations, bizarre delusions, etc.). Adolescents who are dealing with acute concerns surrounding basic sexual identification issues may also find group disclosure extremely difficult, and the other adolescents' own sometimes tenuous sexual identification may raise the group's anxiety to a nonfunctional level.

For the majority of adolescents, group work appears to be the treatment of choice, as either a basic or an adjunct intervention. Group treatment is highly effective in offering opportunities for dealing with the basic tasks of adolescence.

THE SCREENING GROUP

As a measure for assessing the potential for response to group work, and as an introduction to group process, many clinics operate an initial screening group. Adolescents referred to a clinic may participate for five to six sessions in the ongoing screening group where their comfort with group sessions and ability to respond to the group process can be observed. After this experience, they can be referred to long-term groups. One difficulty with this method is that no real group cohesion can develop in such a short time, and the initial group experience may not be entirely positive. When there is a structured method for introducing new members to an ongoing group, new members can usually be easily incorporated.

A disadvantage of this approach is the possibility that an inaccurate estimate of a new member's potential could result in his or her dropping out or needing to be removed from a group. Such a difficult situation needs to be handled carefully to avoid impairment of self-esteem, even if the new member's presence was originally labeled as conditional upon a mutual "good fit."

SELECTION ISSUES
IN RELATION TO GROUP GOALS

Depending on the setting of your group, the therapist may (a) be required to develop groups to meet the general needs of all adolescents referred for group treatment, (b) need to respond to specific problem areas for adolescents in your community, or

(c) have the flexibility for developing groups with individualized goals, and be able to screen for appropriate referrals for those groups.

This book does not address specialized group approaches or programs focused on specific problem areas such as anger control, overeating, and so forth. However, an eclectic, fairly structured adolescent group approach, with both behavioral and insight goals, such as the one described in this book, should be able to utilize the member selection guidelines described.

In addition to the selection criteria described, each adolescent should be able to list at least two problem areas on which they are willing to work in the group. The process of selecting individual goals for group work is described in more detail in the section on therapy contracts and pre-therapy training (Chapter 5).

5

PRE-THERAPY TRAINING, CONTRACTS, AND PRE-THERAPY PREPARATION

Numerous studies with adults have noted the effectiveness of pre-therapy training for increasing the amount and quality of verbal interaction skills (e.g., Gauron & Rawlings, 1975). This may be particularly relevant to adolescent groups, because impaired communication and social skills are often noted as presenting problems which initiate referral to therapy groups (Sugar, 1975). Our own previous research (Corder, Whiteside, & Vogel, 1977) noted a greater initial need for structure and assistance in understanding group process than is typical for adult groups. At that time, very limited research was available which described pre-therapy training programs focused exclusively on the needs of adolescents. Thus, we developed our own pilot programs. Over the years, we have observed that our pre-therapy training develops positive expectations for beneficial effects of treatment, lowers the amount of nonproductive (pastime chatting, low levels of intimacy in verbal output, etc.) time within the adolescent groups, and improves initial patient skills in receiving and giving verbal feedback within the group.

The pre-therapy techniques have been used in outpatient treatment clinics, mental health centers, and a residential hospital program, with both male and female adolescent group members who ranged in age from 13 to 18. These techniques are outlined on the following pages.

TECHNIQUES FOR
GROUP THERAPY PREPARATION

Adolescents referred to us for group therapy are first screened by a review of their records, social history, and previous testing to assess present social functioning, presenting problems, level of reality contact, and impulse control. This may be followed by additional psychological testing, and a minimum of two individual 1-hour screening sessions with the group cotherapists. The adolescent's parents are usually included in one or both of these sessions. The sessions have followed the format shown below:

1. A videotape is shown and discussed. The videotape reviews typical concerns and questions about adolescent groups from adolescents and their parents, gives some details about therapy contracts, and shows an adolescent group session.
2. Written guidelines for giving and receiving verbal feedback within the group are given to the adolescent in a packet. This information is discussed briefly and kept for further review after members have begun the group.
3. A written therapy contract is discussed and signed by parents, the adolescent, and the group therapists.

THE VIDEOTAPE

To develop the videotape, an initial survey of adolescents who had attended therapy groups was made in a number of treatment settings and facilities. The adolescents and their parents were asked to complete a structured questionnaire in which they were asked to list some of their initial concerns, questions, and fears about group membership. Their responses were used as the basis for a 40-minute videotape. It dramatizes an adolescent's first interview with the group therapists, during which these questions and concerns are reviewed. An interview with the adolescent's parents is also shown, illustrating the concerns and issues reflected in parents' responses to the questionnaire. The discussion, development, and signing of a group therapy contract is shown. The contract illustrates mutual understanding and agreement about goals, expectations, group therapy techniques, and confidentiality and is signed by the adolescent patient, his or her parents, and the group therapists.

Then an adolescent group therapy session is dramatized. The session includes good examples of giving and receiving verbal feedback, role-playing, and other group exercises and techniques. Following this segment of the tape, the therapists are shown reviewing the activities of the group and discussing the implications of the group interactions.

DIDACTIC INFORMATION AND GUIDELINES

We have found it helpful to provide written guidelines that describe the characteristics and behaviors we perceive as most effective for group members. These guidelines were modified from those used by Gauron and Rawlings (1975) in pre-therapy training programs for adults. They describe the behaviors which should result in getting the most out of participation in a therapy group. The guidelines emphasize the need for listening to and responding to others, as well as the responsibility for discussing one's own problem areas and working on one's own individual goals in group. The material emphasizes the need for "practice" or continuing to attempt changes in the environment (Corder, 1987, p. 190; see sample on pages 53-54).

THE THERAPY CONTRACT

Two alternative therapy contracts used in two different settings are shown on pages 55 to 58. Each contract needs to be individualized to reflect the needs and constraints of each specific program. However, as noted in Chapter 3, most contracts should address rules of confidentiality and outline expectations and behaviors expected from the group member and his or her parents. It should also describe the group techniques that will be used, along with realistic expectations for changes and results from group participation.

It should list general goals for group membership, along with at least one or two specific, mutually acceptable goals for the prospective adolescent group member, and describe the feedback process used to share any information between therapists, the member's parents, and the treatment facility.

Here are two examples of therapy contracts. The first is reproduced from the author's chapter in *Innovations in Clinical Practice: A Source Book* (Corder, 1987, p. 189).

Another therapy contract which is used by my most frequent collaborator and long-time co-therapist, Dr. Reid Whiteside, is very specific to the setting within which the groups are held.

The Group Therapy Contract (pp. 55-56), which has been used in inpatient and outpatient settings, does not outline the consequences of missing groups and does not list fees. It also does not describe the homework exercises that are often assigned in groups. There has been some negative feedback about the lack of specificity surrounding the description of exceptions from confidentiality rules.

The Adolescent Group Therapy Contract (pp. 57-58) does not describe the techniques used in therapy sessions in any detail. There is also no space for recording the specific goals developed by the adolescent.

Neither contract requires releases for emergency medical treatment. It is unlikely, but possible, that therapists might be required to seek emergency treatment for a group member without being able to contact parents during the emergency. Neither contract outlines all the rule violations which might result in a member's being expelled from a group. A therapy contract is not meant to cover all parameters of treatment nor to cover all possible legal ramifications. The purpose of the contract is to avoid misunderstandings and conflicts by providing a record of the discussion and mutual understanding between clients and therapists of the purposes, techniques, limitations, and goals of therapy.

GROUP PARTICIPATION GUIDELINES

1. It's a waste of time to talk about things concerning yourself that you think are impossible to change ("I can't help my temper . . . that's the way I am"). You can change anything about yourself you really want to change.
2. When someone else is talking, listen and try to understand what they are saying about themselves. It might also apply to you, and they need your view of what they are talking about. This is as much a part of your job as talking about yourself.
3. *Sometimes* suggesting a way of solving a problem is helpful to others. But most of the time, it is more helpful to help them find out why they didn't do the right thing in the first place. People usually know what they should do . . . they just have trouble doing it.
4. You're supposed to practice what you talk about in here. Just talking won't change people much. You have to practice the changes you think about in here in your everyday life. Then be willing to let the group know about how things went when you practiced new ways outside the group.
5. You have an obligation to tell the group about things that are worrying you. The therapists and the group can't read your mind. They will *help* you talk, but you have to make yourself talk about things that concern you.
6. You have an obligation to tell others in the group what you think about the things they say. You have agreed to help each other, and you can do it by telling others in a kind way how they come across to you in the way they act and talk.
7. Try to be as honest as you can. We can't read your mind, and hiding stuff won't help us help you. Try to talk straight about your feelings and thoughts.
8. When something important is happening to you, inside or outside the group, be willing to let the group know about it.

HOW TO TELL OTHER PEOPLE
WHAT YOU THINK ABOUT
WHAT THEY SAY AND DO (GIVING FEEDBACK)

1. Telling someone else what you think can be done in a kind way that is also honest. There's a real difference in attacking someone and in letting them know how they're coming across to you.
2. It's usually better to talk about things you actually see people doing and saying in the group; then you have the real thing to report on.

3. Tell the person how what they did or said made you feel, or what you thought about it without using bad labels (don't say, "You acted like an idiot" or "That was dumb") or name calling. Instead, you might say, "What you did makes me think you were madder than you admit" or "What you said makes me think you were making fun of me and hurt my feelings."
4. Don't talk about people in a general fuzzy way ("He always makes trouble," "She's always like that"). Talk about the actual things they do and say ("You sounded like you did not hear what I said"). Be as specific as you can and don't wait a long time to say what you thought about what is happening in the group.
5. Tell people how you feel about good things you think they say and do. People also need to know when they come across in a good way to others.

HOW TO ACCEPT WHAT OTHERS
SAY TO YOU ABOUT WHAT YOU
SAY AND DO (RECEIVING FEEDBACK)

1. Be willing to talk about what they say to you.
2. Try not to get angry when people have to say things you don't like. You are here to learn how you affect others and how they affect you.
3. You don't have to agree with what people say about you. But you should be willing to accept that this is how it looks and feels to them.
4. If you don't understand what somebody is saying, say so.
5. Ask people to tell you about how they feel about what you do and say. If you take their ideas reasonably, they will be more likely to give them attention.

GROUP THERAPY CONTRACT

This contract is written to help improve understanding, agreement, and communication by (a) the adolescent and the group, (b) parents and guardians, and (c) the therapists, about the goals of therapy, the type of therapy offered, handling of confidential information, and appropriate expectations and responsibilities on the parts of those involved.

Treatment Goals: In group therapy, the adolescent will have the opportunity to learn to talk, think about, and solve problems that he/she agrees to work on with the help of the therapists and the other group members. He/She will be expected to help his/her fellow group members in the same way that they are expected to help him/her. Members are not forced to talk about anything that they do not wish to talk about. Though we cannot work on anything the adolescent is not willing to work on, the group is available to help him/her change the things about himself/herself that he/she does want to change.

For those who are willing to work and try, small changes are usually seen after 12 to 16 sessions (once weekly). Usually people get to know and trust the group and begin talking about important issues in eight sessions. Lasting differences usually don't show up for 6 months to a year; it took people a long time to be the way they are, and it usually takes a while to learn to be a different way. In therapy groups, therapists do not give much direct advice and do not give commands. Rather, they use relationships in the groups and techniques to help people understand themselves, their problems, other people, and the ways that they can go about changing themselves.

Expectations and Responsibilities of Adolescents and Parents: The adolescent is expected to come regularly once a week to the group, to talk about feelings and problems, to listen to others, and to try to help them. If he/she has to miss a session, he/she is expected to call beforehand to give the reason, because others in the group will worry about him/her. He/She has to pick some problem areas to work on, though these may change somewhat later, and be willing to discuss these in the group. Parents and guardians should not expect the group to change anything the adolescent does not want to change, though it often happens that the feedback the person receives from the group will influence him/her to want to change some of the same things parents would like to see him/her change. Parents and guardians will be expected to provide transportation for their adolescent, to pay bills on a regular basis unless the adolescent can agree to take responsibility for paying all or part of his/her bills, and to be involved in collateral parent therapy if this is available. Parents are expected to contact the therapists if they have questions or concerns about the adolescent's experience in therapy.

Confidentiality: Parents will receive letters periodically from the group, written by the therapists, group members, and their adolescent, which tell in general how he/she is getting along and what kinds of things the group thinks it would be helpful for them to know. All specific things said in the group are secret and confidential between the group, and will not be shared with parents unless the adolescent agrees to it. The only exception to this rule is when the adolescent tells something which may result in danger or harm to himself/herself or others. Then the therapists have an obligation to tell parents and/or take other action. The parents can contact the therapists for information or discussion at any time within the limits described.

Individual Goals: Some of the things I want to work on in the group are (adolescent writes in own goals statements and must select at least two goals):

We have read and understand and agree with the therapy plan described.

SIGNED:

_____   _____
Parent/Guardian   Date

_____   _____
Parent/Guardian   Date

_____   _____
Adolescent   Date

_____   _____
Therapist   Date

_____   _____
Therapist   Date

ADOLESCENT GROUP
THERAPY CONTRACT

1. *Initial Time Commitment*: A reasonable amount of time is required in order to get the feel of how group treatment can help. I AGREE TO ATTEND THE INITIAL SIX SESSIONS, AND UNDERSTAND THAT I WILL BE CHARGED FOR SIX SESSIONS if I should discontinue before my initial commitment is completed.

2. *Attendance*: Group members quickly become significant to each other. Because of the importance of commitment and consistency, group members must commit to attend all group meetings punctually. Because this time has been reserved exclusively for the group, I UNDERSTAND THAT OFFICE POLICY REQUIRES THAT I PAY FOR ANY MISSED SESSION, REGARDLESS OF THE REASON. Members will be notified when the entire group is canceled from time to time to coincide with major school vacations, and temporary withdrawals may be made.

3. *Stopping Group*: Treatment goals are identified at the beginning by the group member, parents, and group leaders. Periodically the member receives feedback from the group and therapists about his or her progress toward treatment goals. Recommendation for termination is made when there is consistent agreement about satisfactory completion of the individual's goals. There is no set minimum beyond the initial six sessions. However, *it is necessary for members to give 2 full weeks' notice of their intention to stop group.* I UNDERSTAND THAT I MUST ATTEND OR PAY FOR THE TWO SESSIONS FOLLOWING MY ANNOUNCEMENT THAT I INTEND TO STOP GROUP. This is very important in order to consolidate gains and to say goodbyes.

4. *Payments*: Monthly statements must show a zero balance. Payments can be made in advance for the month, paid weekly at the time of sessions, or the charges for the month may be paid in full on the last session of the month.

   The only exception to this rule is for members covered by HMO insurance companies (see attached rules for your specific HMO).

5. *Confidentiality*: In order for the group to feel safe, group members must trust that their confidentiality will be protected. I AGREE NOT TO DISCUSS OUTSIDE OF THE GROUP ANYTHING SAID BY MY FELLOW MEMBERS DURING SESSIONS. I MAY DISCUSS ONLY MY WORK AND THE COMMENTS OF THE GROUP LEADERS.

6. *Parent Collateral Meetings*: Group leaders will meet with parents on a regular basis. It is important for parents to know how therapy is progressing, and to have input into treatment. At the same time, group leaders must protect confidentiality in order to encourage open and honest discussion in therapy. Group leaders will therefore

use their own judgment about what to disclose or keep private. Some illicit or illegal activities may not be disclosed. There are exceptions: Group leaders must notify parents or proper authorities if there are indications that the patient seriously intends to injure himself/herself or others, or if child abuse is suspected.

In order for group therapy to be effective, regular collaboration with parents is essential. I AGREE TO ATTEND INDIVIDUAL PARENT COLLATERAL SESSIONS WITH GROUP LEADERS AT LEAST ONCE EVERY 6 WEEKS. Sometimes child management problems or family conflicts may necessitate more frequent involvement. Recommendations for psychological or medical evaluation will be made if indicated.

7. *Relationships and Homework*: The support provided by peers and practice in interpersonal skills is an important part of treatment. Group members may be encouraged to call each other between sessions. Dating and romance between group members can be disruptive to treatment, however, and members should bring all emotionally important material back to the group for informal discussion and exploration.

8. *Time and Fees*: Fee for this group is $_____, and the length of the session is 90 minutes.   This group meets from

_____.

9. *To Parents:* Supervision can only be provided during the times groups are meeting. Please be available to bring and pick up adolescents on time. PLEASE CALL ANY TIME YOU HAVE ANY CONCERNS, QUESTIONS, OR SUGGESTIONS. With parent support, group therapy can be a very positive experience for adolescents.

SIGNED:

_____   _____
Group Member   Date

_____   _____
Parent/Guardian   Date

_____   _____
Parent/Guardian   Date

_____   _____
Group Therapist   Date

_____   _____
Group Therapist   Date

REFERENCES

Corder, B. F. (1987). Planning and leading adolescent therapy groups. In P. A. Keller & S. R. Heyman (Eds.), *Innovations in Clinical Practice: A Source Book* (Vol. 6, pp. 177-196). Sarasota, FL: Professional Resource Exchange.

Corder, B. F., Whiteside, R., & Vogel, M. (1977). A therapeutic game for structuring and facilitating group process. *Adolescence, 17,* 261-286.

Gauron, E., & Rawlings, K. (1975). A procedure for orienting new members to group psychotherapy. *Small Group Behavior, 3,* 293-307.

Sugar, M. (Ed.). (1975). *The Adolescent in Group and Family Therapy.* New York: Brunner/Mazel.

6

GIVING FEEDBACK TO PARENTS AND OTHERS

Within the limits of confidentiality for group members, it is probably a safe statement that most parents want as much direct feedback about the adolescent's group participation as possible. In addition, an earlier chapter has outlined the legal advantages of providing continuing feedback about program participation to parents, to avoid misunderstandings and unrealistic expectations for the treatment program. Many clinic settings use the "child guidance model" of a separate therapist for child and parent. The primary disadvantage for this model is the added staff time and fees involved, as well as the communication distance between the group therapists and their feedback to parents about group process.

An alternative approach is to have group therapists meet at intervals with adolescent member's parents. However, it may not be possible for some therapists to add these collaborative meetings to their present caseload. Still another approach consists of having collaborative parent groups meeting either with the adolescent group therapists, or in a separate parent therapy group. However, with this approach, parents have sometimes complained about lack of time for individual focus on their own child and on specific problem-solving techniques uniquely related to their own situation.

The author and co-workers have used many different combinations of these approaches and prefer to meet with each group member's parents at intervals, and have each parent take turns joining the adolescent group for at least one session, using the "Parent Hot Seat" techniques described in Chapter 9. In summary, this consists of the following process: (a) Each adolescent group member outlines specific problem areas with parents as part of the group process, (b) the group responds with questions and lists of concerns about the adolescent's interactions with parents and environment, (c) a list of these questions and topics is drawn up by the group, who also assign a "Parent Protector" to handle the interchange in the "Parent Hot Seat" session, (d) a "Member Protector" is assigned to handle any excessive stress or anxiety for the group member during the session, and (e) parents attend the group and present their perception of the issues brought up by the group, explore possible approaches and compromises, and are asked to make positive statements about their adolescent as well as listing their continuing concerns.

A variety of types of written feedback have been explored by the author. One example of a structured letter used for feedback to parents and administrators in facility settings is shown on pages 64 to 66. Notes for the letter are taken by the therapists, who complete one section of the form in the group using feedback from group members, and share their own evaluations of the members with the group in the second section. During the group assessment period, the group members also verbalize their self-assessment of their progress and participation.

Although we request verbal input from parents, the "return forms" on pages 67 to 68 from parents, to share with the adolescent and group, may also be helpful.

SCHOOL LIAISON AND
FEEDBACK WITH OTHER AGENCIES

Unless the adolescent has also been assigned a case administrator, or group therapy is an adjunct treatment along with individual therapy, the group therapist is faced with the responsibility for a number of environmental interventions and liaisons. Group members may make remarkable shifts in attitude toward school, but may still be quite delayed in their academic skills and require intensive remedial work. The need for extracurricular activities and specific planning for them is a problem for many members who need more structure in their environment.

Exploration of attitudes about and options for birth-control planning with parents and physicians may require at least some initial information exchange with the therapists.

The most impressive gains in skills monitored by group process must be buttressed by these types of environmental interventions. Most therapists will need to plan for these types of liaison work. This means significant amounts of time for scheduling sessions, phone calls, and so forth. My own experience has been that these issues are some of the most draining and demanding of therapists' time, when there is no liaison staff or case administrator to handle them. This is probably one of the main reasons why there are fewer adolescent groups than adult groups operating in the private practice sector. The investment of time and energy necessary often results in minimized financial rewards for the therapist.

To be effective, therapists must develop a library of information related to local programs for a wide range of supportive experiences for adolescents. These may include extracurricular programs to build self-esteem, develop feelings of mastery, and structure their after-school and summer hours in some creative fashion. In our own practice, this has involved investigating the merits and reputation of local drama schools, modeling schools, and martial arts programs as well as programs for remedial and alternative education.

If the group therapists are meeting in alternate collaborative sessions with parents, this repertoire of information is invaluable. It may also be crucial for therapists to have an extensive knowledge of the local rules and regulations within the county or city school system. It is often necessary to assist parents in changing a youth's school placement, locating schools with appropriate remedial programs, and requesting special dispensation from normal school requirements for teens who may require a brief psychiatric hospitalization or other special consideration.

THE EVALUATION LETTER

DEAR TREATMENT TEAM
AND PARENTS OR GUARDIANS:

    As a report to you about how group therapy is progressing, we will be sending you this letter every _____ weeks. The letter will be filled out by the group therapist, the adolescent group members, and by your own adolescent. We will be checking about general areas of concern and about progress on their individual goals. No confidential group material will be included. As we have previously agreed, any information about possible self-harm or destructive behavior towards others, is excluded from rules about confidentiality. If you have any questions about this letter, please contact _____ at _____. All conferences about the letter will also be discussed with the group member concerned.

TO BE COMPLETED BY GROUP THERAPISTS:

In general he/she shows, by his/her level of involvement and participation in group:

_____

_____

Within the group and with other young people in the group, he/she shows the following level of frequency of verbal input to the group:

_____

_____

Response to limit-setting in the group:

_____

_____

Ability to give and receive feedback from the group:

_____

_____

Ability to discuss and deal with everyday problems:

_____

_____

Ability to bring up and discuss things which are truly important to him/her:

_____

_____

Ability to understand responsibility for his/her own behavior:

_____

_____

OTHER COMMENTS:

TO BE COMPLETED BY THE GROUP MEMBERS WITH ASSIS-
TANCE OF THERAPISTS (check item which best describes member
from one of the two columns):

Shows Good Achievement	Needs Improvement
____ Prompt, on time.	____ Seldom on time.
____ Polite and attentive.	____ Interrupts others, is impolite
____ Gives feedback to others in helpful way.	____ Criticizes others in hurtful way.
____ Talks about important things.	____ Does too much playing and chitchat.
____ Is willing to talk about feelings.	____ Does not talk about feelings.
____ Shows "adult" behavior most of time in group.	____ Shows immature behavior in group.

OTHER COMMENTS:

TO BE COMPLETED BY GROUP MEMBER INDIVIDUALLY:

Of the specific problem areas which I selected to work on in the group, I
feel I have been working on:

_____

_____

I can describe how I think I have been doing in the group as:

_____

_____

The things I want to continue working on in the group are:

_____

_____

Some things I would like to work on changing at home are:

_____

_____

SIGNED:

_____   _____
Group Member   Date

_____   _____
Therapist   Date

PARENT RESPONSE FORM

DATE: _____

TO: _____, Therapists, and other members of the
            adolescent therapy group.

I/WE HAVE READ YOUR LAST LETTER AND WOULD LIKE TO
MAKE THE FOLLOWING COMMENTS:

I/We would describe my/our own perception of _____'s behavior
at home and school as:

_____

_____

The following are changes I/we see at home and school since I/we received your last letter:

_____

_____

The things I/we feel best about him/her are:

_____

_____

The things I/we still have some concerns about are:

_____

_____

The thing I/we would most like to see him/her work on in the group is:

_____

_____

The thing I/we would like most to have suggestions on handling from
the group and therapist is:

_____

_____

The thing I/we feel that I/we need the most understanding and help from
him/her on is:

_____

_____

A nice, positive thing I/we would like to say about him/her to the group
and to him/her is:

_____

_____

ADDITIONAL COMMENTS, CONCERNS, COMPLIMENTS, AND
SO ON:

SIGNED:

_____   _____
Parent/Guardian   Date

_____   _____
Parent/Guardian   Date

7

PRE- AND POST-TESTING FOR ADOLESCENT GROUPS

It is critical to develop some measures of progress in your adolescent group, both from an administrative standpoint, and as an assessment of the effectiveness of the group intervention for individual members. Unfortunately, many commercially available instruments are not sensitive to some of the specific goals that may be the focus of an individual's treatment, and they are not likely to reflect the presence or absence in the group of some of the critical curative factors described earlier. Many therapists develop their own pre- and post-test instruments to insure that the specific goals for their groups can be measured. Here are some examples of the types of measures that we often use in adolescent therapy groups. They focus on the specific goals listed by the adolescent, the presenting problem areas described by parents, and the assessment of the functioning of the individual *within* the group. (See pre-/post-evaluation instrument on pages 72-73.)

Although this simple pre- and post-test does not begin to measure many subtle changes that may occur in group therapy, it may measure some of the areas related to the curative factors described earlier. It does, however, speak to changes in specific goals and problem areas identified by adolescents and their parents.

Among the many measures that we have found to be an effective supplement to our own test are the Tennessee Self

Concept Scale (Fitts, 1974) and the Devereux Adolescent Behavior Rating Scale (Spivack, Spotts, & Haimes, 1967).

Whatever instrument you choose to assess the functioning in your group, it is critical to have some fairly objective measure of progress for administrative use and for your own professional growth. Using some of the co-therapy collaboration measures discussed in Chapter 2, you should be able to identify absences of any curative factors, and identify group members who may need more focus or additional interventions. This measurement can also help you plan research projects by emphasizing specific needs and deficits in your group approach and techniques.

ADDITIONAL INSTRUMENTS
TO MEASURE
SOCIAL SKILLS DEVELOPMENT

Other instruments that have been used to measure social skills development and which might be useful in assessing the effects of group intervention will be discussed next.

ADOLESCENT PROBLEMS INVENTORY
(Freedman et al., 1978)

In this test, 44 problem situations are used. The scene, characters, history, and goals in the problem situation are read aloud, and the subjects are asked to pick the "best response" among multiple-choice alternatives. This test was developed originally for use with males only, and the limitations of the range of interpersonal environments illustrated has been noted. Because it was developed to differentiate between delinquent and nondelinquent populations, it may lack the ability to measure more subtle changes in better functioning group members.

MULTIPLE-CHOICE PROBLEM INVENTORY
FOR GIRLS (MCPIFG; Gaffney, 1984)

This instrument for measuring girls' social competence requires the test taker to describe her probable response to a series of described interpersonal conflicts. These responses are rated along a 5-point scale, and scores indicate similarities of the respondent's perceived behavior to that of delinquent populations. Again, this type of inventory would probably require some supplemental information from others in the environment to measure actual behavior changes, but it should be able to evaluate intellectual grasp of acceptable behavior alternatives in interpersonal conflict situations.

TEST OF ADOLESCENT SOCIAL SKILLS
KNOWLEDGE (Whiteside, 1987)

Whiteside has developed the Test of Adolescent Social Skills Knowledge (TASSK), which measures social skills and social judgment of normal adolescents. This test measures the problem-solving skills of youth in dealing with interpersonal conflicts. It requires the youths to make judgments about the best solution to a number of conflict situations. The booklet illustrates a variety of conflict scenarios with four possible alternative resolutions. The solution which best describes their own behavior is chosen. The solutions chosen yield scores showing the individual's tendency to ascribe social behaviors to themselves which may be characterized as:

1. Appropriate - effective and healthy social responses to the scenario described.
2. Defiant - primarily aggressive and antisocial responses which confront authority.
3. Avoidant - tendencies to avoid confrontation, or to isolate themselves socially.
4. Misguided - ineffective, poor problem solving likely to be perceived as immature or irrational.

The advantage of this measure is that it has been given to a fairly large normative sample and compares well in reliability and validity with other more widely used scales. The disadvantage is that it measures the respondent's *perception* of his or her behavior and should probably be supplemented by some other measure of observed behavior in the environment (teacher, parent ratings, etc.).

CORDER-WHITESIDE
PRE- / POST- *(Circle One)* EVALUATION
ADOLESCENT GROUP

NAME:_____   DATE:_____

THERAPISTS: Corder and Whiteside

Pre-Group / Post-Group
Test of Problem and Skill Areas

Problem	Frequency (how many times per day, week, month):_____
Argument/Conflict With Parents	Day____ Week ____ Month____
In-School Suspension	Day____ Week ____ Month____
Smoking Pot	Day____ Week ____ Month____

GOAL STATEMENTS: Reduce amount of conflict with parents, have no in-school suspensions, and reduce dependence on smoking pot.

Level of Skill Rating to Use

5 = Effective, Consistent
4 = Effective, Inconsistent
3 = Beginning to be Demonstrated
2 = Needs Improvement
1 = Severely Deficient

Interpersonal Skills Demonstrated	Level of Skill Rating
Ability to verbalize and express feelings.	
Ability to give feedback to others in group.	
Ability to take and use feedback from others.	
Willingness to try behavior changes.	

Interpersonal Skills Demonstrated	Level of Skill Rating
Ability to make positive statements about self.	
Ability to show basic age-appropriate social skills.	
Ability and willingness to control anger.	
Attempts to communicate and interact with others outside group.	
Shows no obvious substance dependency.	
Makes effort to achieve in school.	
Interacts positively with parents.	

Problem-Solving Skills Demonstrated	Level of Skill Rating
Ability to view problem from all sides.	
Ability to verbalize problem areas in conflicts.	
Ability to express needs in polite, positive manner.	
Ability to suggest solutions.	
Ability to compensate others for compromise.	
Ability to handle compromise.	

REFERENCES

Fitts, W. H. (1974). *Tennessee Self Concept Scale*. Nashville, TN: Counselor Recordings and Tests.

Freedman, B., Rosenthal, L., Donahoe, C., Schlundt, D., & McFail, M. (1978). A social-behavioral analysis of skills deficits in delinquent and nondelinquent adolescent boys. *Journal of Consulting and Clinical Psychology, 46,* 1448-1462.

Gaffney, L. R. (1984). A multiple-choice test to measure social skills in delinquent and nondelinquent adolescent girls. *Journal of Consulting and Clinical Psychology, 52,* 911-912.

Spivack, G., Spotts, J., & Haimes, P. (1967). *Devereux Adolescent Behavior Rating Scale*. Devon, PA: The Devereux Foundation.

Whiteside, R. (1987). *Development and Validation of an Illustrated Multiple Choice Test of Social Skills Knowledge of Adolescents*. Unpublished doctoral dissertation, North Carolina State University, Raleigh, NC. Additional information may be obtained from Whiteside and Daniel Associates, 4301 Lake Boone Trail, Raleigh, NC 27607 (Telephone: 919-783-8829).

8

THE GROUP PROCESS

BEGINNING PHASES
OF THE GROUP

Beginning sessions of many adolescent groups are characterized by fairly high anxiety levels manifested in some giggling,
nervous movements, "contagious silliness," and difficulty in getting down to the business of the group. In the early sessions, patients are self-focused and tend to have less skill at responding
to the needs of others, or in responding to topics which are initiated by others. The structured groups described in this book
tend to decrease many of these behaviors by providing a concrete structure for encouraging group input and feedback.
Group members begin to test confidentiality by tentatively sharing information about their environment and behavior outside
the group. They tend to give more negative feedback than positive feedback to others in the group before strong group cohesion develops. The general tasks of the group leader in this
stage of structured groups are to (a) encourage group input by
modeling behaviors, or by providing structured techniques; (b)
monitor and handle the group's anxiety level; (c) modify group
verbalizations when necessary to protect self-esteem of individual members and allow a sense of safety to develop within the
group; (d) model and encourage the examination of verbal content and group process behavior, the first steps in development
of insight; and (f) teach members to handle the various "roles"
assigned.

In these early sessions, the group learns to share group time so that each member can participate, to respond with "feeling statements" rather than judgmental ones (feedback input and output), and to begin to model the therapist's verbal process and interactions with the group. The group must be encouraged to establish its originality by setting its own rules and developing its own shared group goals. Individual goals should be written into pre-therapy contracts, but these may be expanded into shared group goals. In our experience, all these tasks are taught more effectively in our structured groups by the literal assignment of "roles" to group members. These various roles mirror the group's tasks and gradually allow the group to handle some of the therapists' functions. Roles are defined as Rules Enforcer, Encourager, Member Protector, and so on.

MIDDLE PHASES OF THE GROUP

Middle phase work in most groups takes place after the development of adequate group cohesion and the development of fairly deep levels of intimacy among group members. At this point, group members should be capable of demonstrating sufficient skills in giving and receiving feedback to allow an easy flow of interchange, some confrontation, and mutual sharing of experiences.

The leaders' role involves keeping the group on task, encouraging the group to find shared themes in their separate experiences, teaching negotiation skills, and helping the group members to explore their feelings and responses beyond simple cathartic levels. In the structured adolescent group, there are requirements for concentration on some individual goals for each member. The mastery of these goals involves shared group work on a number of exercises, followed by group and individual assessment of progress toward these goals. In the structured adolescent group, members are expected to involve their parents in some sessions for practice and work on negotiation exercises. Other exercises may allow for more intense confrontation with members about their behavior and its consequences.

"Homework" will be more complex and demanding in these types of groups and includes reports to the group on success and difficulties. More complex role assignments are made in the structured adolescent group as the members demonstrate more capacity for insight, more adequate verbal skills, and have had more opportunity to carry out functions modeled by therapists. This can be seen in role labels like Other Side Viewer, Consequencer, Inside Voice, and so forth.

LATER PHASES OF THE GROUP

In middle to later phases of the group, alliances among members which have developed will deepen, and some difficulties in controlling inappropriate affiliations or sexual contacts outside the group may develop. Generally, there is a deepening of intimacy and cohesion among all group members which becomes a satisfying and supportive factor in their lives. Members take more and more control of the group process, and in our structured groups begin to make suggestions about using exercises, role-play, and other techniques. Members who have reached their goals and continue in the group as peer mentors may be asked to assume responsibility for some of the therapist's earlier functions (assigning roles, designing role-play scenarios, etc.). As other members reach their goals and prepare to leave the group, leave-taking ceremonies are carried out which offer opportunities for practice and mastery of interpersonal skills. This phase is characterized by synthesis and drill in members' mastery of interpersonal relations, problem solving, and development of insight into their behavior patterns.

RESPONDING TO PROBLEM BEHAVIORS

This discussion begins with the assumption that co-therapists have addressed the various cooperative issues covered in Chapter 2, which outlines therapists' role and function, and collaborative work between therapists. Some common problem areas and the approaches we have used to handle them in structured adolescent groups are as follows:

1. *How do you assess and control a group's level of anxiety?* Heightened activity levels and motoric agitation in the group or, conversely, lengthening silences and a decrease in verbal output, may be signs of increased stress levels. Giggling, silliness, and forays into "pastime" discussions are other indications that some interventions from group leaders may be needed. After an ex-

ploration of the basis for the increased tension, therapists may introduce some role-play exercises or structured techniques described in earlier chapters. With increased structure, members are not acutely pressured for
spontaneous interactions and are able to reorganize their
responses within a less stressful framework.

2. *How would you handle a group member who verbally
   monopolizes sessions?* Before the verbal flow of the
   monopolizer becomes a problem, it is helpful for leaders to interrupt by saying, "These are important issues.
   Let's get some feedback from others in the group about
   how they are understanding them and what feelings
   they can share with you." This type of behavior appears to be less problematic in our structured groups
   because there are roles assigned for each member, and
   because techniques such as "Member Hot Seat" allow
   periodic examination of behaviors which might be po-
   tentially disruptive to the group.

3. *How would you handle a group member's being scapegoated?* Scapegoating tends to occur when a member's
   functioning is deviant from group norms and when a
   member is unable to participate effectively in group interactions. Structured assignment of roles allows each
   member to make some important input into the group
   and provides a framework for teaching them to make
   that input. This structure decreases the probability of a
   member's being left out, or appearing unable to contrib-
   ute to the group interactions. If a particular group member appears to be attacking or confronting another member in a highly focused manner, it is possible to put the
   attacker on the "Member Hot Seat" and to allow the
   group to examine their motives and hostile behavior.

4. *How would you handle a group member who becomes
   physically aggressive?* Rules against physical aggression are typically included in the group rules developed
   in initial sessions. If a member cannot follow these
   rules, after being warned by the Rules Enforcer member, one of the co-therapists will usually ask the agi-
   tated member to leave the group with him or her, allowing the group to continue with the other therapist. After
   the causes of the attempted aggression are explored
   briefly, expelled members are given an opportunity to
   reorganize their behavior and allowed to return to the

group if they feel they can handle their behavior and help to explore the causes with the group. If they are unable to do this, they will be expelled from the group for the remainder of the session.

5. *How would you handle a group member who is withdrawn and does not speak during a group session?* This probably could not happen in our structured groups, because each member is assigned a specific role to carry out in the session. If individuals seem to be having more than usual difficulty with roles or verbalization, other group members may be assigned to assist them as their "Member Protector" for that session. This formalized support and encouragement from a specific group member has proven to be very effective.

6. *How do you handle a group member's suddenly becoming upset and dashing from a room?* As with an aggressive outburst, one therapist would leave to help the member handle his or her feelings and behavior while the remaining therapist helps the group explore their ideas and feelings about the incident. Usually the member is able to return to the group where he or she can give and receive feedback about his or her actions.

7. *How would you respond to an acutely disturbed group member's verbalizing confused or psychotic ideation in the group?* Initially, the therapists and group would respond by reframing any irrational statements in a caring but reality-based manner ("We know that this seems real to you, but to us it does not seem real or logical. It seems as if you are under stress, and your thinking seems to be getting mixed up and confused"). Additional group support might be added with the assignment of a "Member Protector." If the member were to continue with these verbalizations in other sessions, we might suggest that he or she work in individual therapy until the therapist felt he or she was able to handle the group process. Some group members have had to be hospitalized occasionally, and the group has continued to be quite supportive, calling on them at the hospital, sending notes and cards from the group, and encouraging their return after the hospitalization. Although decompensation of a member is very anxiety provoking to the group, most groups can discuss their concerns and understand the process by which stress levels overcome

defense mechanisms. Their supportive actions and communication with the disturbed member can also facilitate a feeling of altruism, which has been identified as a curative factor in adolescent groups.

8. *How would you handle sexual acting out between group members that is reported within the group?* This would be dealt with in essentially the same manner as other inappropriate behavior which violates rules of the group. The members may be assigned to a "Member Hot Seat" role, where they explore consequences and motivations for the acting-out behavior, and some negotiation for change would be attempted.

9. *How would you deal with sexually explicit material brought out in the group?* Understanding and dealing with sexuality is one of the basic tasks of adolescence. Rules for verbalization of any topic are set by the group in their initial group sessions. If a member's verbalizations are primitive and unacceptable, such as deliberately lewd labeling of sexual anatomy or descriptions of sexual acts, the therapists will intervene to restate the group rules about inappropriate language, and help the members reframe some of their concerns or feelings in a more acceptable manner. If the behavior continues, and the group's anxiety level appears to interrupt the group process in a significant manner, the therapists may ask that some particularly anxiety-provoking material be handled with the therapists outside the group. Questions or concerns about alternative behaviors or problem solving can be brought back into the group without the sharing of explicit details.

10. *How do you deal with complaints and highly negative statements made in the group against the facility, other staff members, or one of the present therapists?* We would use similar techniques to handle most problem or acting-out behaviors. The therapists would allow an appropriate verbalization of feelings, explore underlying problem areas, and then lead the group through the problem-solving and negotiating steps which are described in Chapter 9. The basic difference in our structured adolescent group and other groups is the prior assignment of member roles which encourage and teach group members to share the therapists' responsibilities. Chapter 9 describes the member roles which would be

important in this example, including the "Other Side Viewer," who would be asked to describe the problem from the perspective of the facility or staff, and the "Consequencer," who gives ideas about the possible consequences of the member's attitude and behavior.

11. *How would you deal with a member's sharing excessively sensitive material too early in the group process, such as beginning to discuss incest experiences in the first group session?* It is typically socially inappropriate to share details of intimate experiences before developing a relationship with others. One of the goals of the group is to teach and practice social skills. The therapists would limit the amount of disclosure, respond to some of the feelings from both the member and group, and suggest that, "We will be able to be more helpful to you in talking about this after we get to know you better, and after you know others in the group better. If you feel you need to talk about this immediately, you can talk to us (co-therapists) after the group session. Then we can decide what parts of your feelings and thoughts the group will be able to help you with in the sessions."

Group members are allowed to initiate any subject for discussion in the group, and most groups can handle some aspects of most problem areas. Whether a specific group can handle an anxiety-provoking experience such as this depends on the explicitness of the verbalized details, the current group cohesion and intimacy levels, and the amount of practice the group has had in dealing with difficult problem areas.

12. *If some members are involved in other types of therapy, how can group experiences be integrated into their treatment?* Some individual therapists feel that group membership may dilute the individual therapy experience. They may refer clients to group only after they feel maximum benefit has been reached in individual therapy, or when they feel the client's primary problems are in the interpersonal relationship sphere.

Other group therapists may add occasional individual sessions to deal with issues which the client may feel are too sensitive to handle in group (e.g., pregnancy, incest). When individual therapy sessions involve a therapist other than the group leaders, added dimensions of complexity must be addressed through collaborative sessions for the therapists.

13. *How do you handle members entering and leaving the group?* In our structured groups, new members are paired with an experienced group member, who may meet with them briefly before the group, and will "introduce" them to the group. The assignment of structured roles allows the new member to enter the group interaction in a directed, nonthreatening fashion. Members who are leaving the group are asked to make a "Legacy Tape" which lists the things they learned about themselves from the group and describes the positive things they felt about being in the group. They are asked to give the new member taking their place in the group some suggestions about how to use the group and how to function effectively in the group. Our members have used these tapes creatively, sometimes including original music or poems, and usually leaving some personal messages for each of the remaining group members. In some groups members prepare a "Legacy Book" for the departing member with messages, poems, and photos, listing the changes they had seen, giving positive feedback, and describing any areas on which the member should continue to work.

9

STRUCTURED ROLE ASSIGNMENT IN ADOLESCENT GROUPS

As noted in earlier chapters, our previous research on curative factors (Corder, Whiteside, & Haizlip, 1981) found that adolescents tend to express more satisfaction with group experiences that they perceive as offering adequate opportunities for these curative factors to develop. The selected curative factors perceived as most helpful for adolescents are (a) learning how to express feelings, (b) giving and receiving feedback about how they are perceived and how they perceive others, and (c) feeling that they are part of a group where they are accepted and able to share feelings and experiences in a caring manner. Given time, most groups will develop the cohesion and interpersonal exchange necessary for providing these opportunities. Any technique for insuring that these opportunities develop as rapidly as possible would be helpful in adolescent groups, given their rapid shifts in process and the adolescent's limited ability to handle high group levels of anxiety, extended silences, and so on (Corder, Haizlip, & Walker, 1980). When progress toward these goals is too slow, it has been our experience that adolescent members may not continue their participation in the group long enough to develop the interpersonal relationships and exchanges that underlie the development of curative factors.

To increase the probability of developing curative factors, and deal with the inherently high anxiety levels present in the initial phases of adolescent groups, we have developed a repertoire of techniques used to structure adolescent psychotherapy groups. We have used our techniques with adolescents aged 13 to 18 in settings that include group homes, mental health centers, hospital inpatient units, and private outpatient services.

In addition to facilitating the development of curative factors, we have found that the use of these structures has allowed us to include a number of fairly nonverbal oppositional patients in a group. The structure also has been helpful in avoiding scapegoating of members who are deviant from the group norms in behavior or level of social sophistication. At the same time, the structures have appeared flexible enough to allow a fairly spontaneous flow of group process, which is one requirement for insight work in groups.

STRUCTURING TECHNIQUES - EARLY GROUP SESSIONS

In beginning the groups, we have modified a number of commonly used encounter-group techniques to lower initial anxiety levels and introduce the members to each other in a relaxed manner. At the first group meeting, members are randomly paired, sent to the edges of the room in pairs, and asked to find the following information out about each other: (a) name, age, school, age of siblings; (b) three things they particularly like (such as hobbies, music groups, extracurricular activities, etc.); (c) at least one reason why they had been referred for group therapy (or something their parents, school counselor, etc. had described as a reason); and (d) any particular questions they had in their own mind about what it would be like being in a group like this one. After these brief pairings the group comes together, and the pairs take turns "introducing" each other to the group. Particularly for lower functioning groups, it may be helpful to have the instructions for this exercise written out on a blackboard or poster. During the introductions, the group is instructed to, "Ask anyone anything else you'd like to know about them, as long as it is something you'd ask anyone else when you were first getting to know them."

As an icebreaker, and to help the group remember first names, a "ball game" may be used. A Ping-Pong or foam ball is tossed randomly around the group while each member says his or her own name, then names another person and tosses him or her the ball; speed is gradually increased until it reaches the group limits.

LISTING GROUP AND INDIVIDUAL GOALS

In their initial contract, members had listed a minimum of one goal on which they will focus their work in the group. These goals, and two others, if possible, are listed by each group member and written out on poster boards which are taped to walls for each session. At times during the group session, these goals are very useful for reference, assessment of progress, and, occasionally, for confrontation around the member's level of involvement and work toward change. Some examples of goals listed by members are: "Getting along better with my parents," "Not being suspended at school anymore," "Not being so shy," and "Figuring out whether I want to live with my mother or my father."

Each member is also given a "Goal Book" which is used later in a number of group exercises, including records of the group's assessment of member progress. These are described in more detail in a later section.

BEHAVIORAL RULES AND EXPECTATIONS FOR GROUP PARTICIPATION

Group rules for expected behavior are developed during these initial sessions by the group members and recorded on a poster displayed during each session. These rules typically include the group's decisions about smoking, descriptions of what they consider acceptable parameters of language used in mixed company, reminders about confidentiality, procedures for excused absences, and some outline of expectations for group participation. If there has been no pre-therapy training, the group leaders may add some requirements for giving and receiving feedback. An example of the group rules from one of our author and co-worker's groups follows:

1. If you have to miss group, you must call the leaders or the "Group Contractor" to let them know the reasons why, so we won't worry about you. Everybody is supposed to come to every meeting unless they're out-of-town or there's an emergency.
2. Everybody has to try every exercise at least once.

3. Everybody has to at least try to do any "homework" assigned.
4. When you let someone know what you think about something they say or do, you do not label them or their behavior (dumb, stupid, etc.). You can let them know how it makes you feel and what you think might happen as a result of their behavior, and you can let them know how you think other people will feel about their behavior.
5. You will listen to other people and try to help them in the group too.
6. Nobody should come to the group impaired (stoned, drinking, etc.).
7. Everybody should try to be honest in what they say.
8. There should be no talk about what happens in the group to anyone outside the group. (*Exception*: If anybody talks about hurting themselves or someone else.)
9. Smoking is okay if your parents allow smoking ("If you can't smoke other places, you can't smoke in group").
10. If you leave the group for any reason, you have to tell the group why you're leaving and come back to the group two last times to let the group say goodbye.

HOMEWORK

In many sessions, individual members or the whole group may be assigned homework, which typically consists of a requirement for practicing some behavior (negotiation, anger control) outside the group. When homework is assigned, members must report back to the group and have their performance "graded."

THE NEW LEARNING GAME

This is a therapeutic game, evolved from a previous version (Corder, Whiteside, & Vogel, 1977) used in a variety of settings to structure early group sessions and facilitate group interaction with difficult, resistive group members. The purpose of the newer version is to provide enjoyable and informative practice in verbal expressions of feelings and to aid the development of communication and interaction skills (Corder, in press).

There is a simple game board around which members move their game pieces, after rolling dice. They then select cards from the stacks indicated by the section of the game board on which they "land" after rolling the dice. The cards are divided into three categories labeled "Learning About Yourself," "Learning About Others," and "Learning How to Solve Problems." The items in each category are divided into levels of difficulty and amount of group cohesion typically needed to complete the task. Each of the items has been developed to deal with some aspect of the typical tasks of adolescence.

At times, the therapists have deliberately "stacked the deck" to make certain that a particular item with specific relevance to a group member or the current group process will be among the cards chosen. Examples of the cards are shown below.

Learning About Yourself. "Describe some conflict with your parents which keeps happening over and over again without anyone finding a solution."

Learning About Others. "Describe the things which you think are the most important in choosing a friend (of the opposite sex), and tell why those things are important to you."

Learning How to Solve Problems. "You want to go to the beach for a weekend with a friend and use a house that belongs to a friend's relative. There is no chaperone. Act out how you would try to negotiate this with your parents and show what compromise you would probably make to reach a solution."

The purpose of the game is to encourage discussion rather than completing or winning the game. Each item typically adds instructions to: "Ask the person on your right to answer the same question," "Ask a person of the opposite sex to answer the same question," or "Have every person in the group answer this same question." At times, a whole session has been centered around the group's response to a single game item.

CONTINUING AND MIDDLE
PHASES OF GROUP PROCESS

ASSIGNING MEMBER ROLES

In most group process, members gradually assume some of the functions of the group leaders, displaying the supportive, clarifying, and other behaviors that are modeled by the group leaders. In order to speed this process, and to allow members who seem more passive or shy to assume some of these active roles, as well as affording an opportunity for rotating and "trying out" new roles, a variety of group roles are randomly assigned at the beginning of each session. Each member is given some role or responsibility for that session.

The roles are assigned randomly by having members take plastic pins labeled with the name of the roles from a covered basket. Members wear their labels for the session. There may be some occasions when a member takes multiple roles and wears several role buttons. Some roles are highly specialized to function in specific group exercises and will be described later.

Rules Enforcer. The Rules Enforcer identifies any rule violations and asks the group to deal with any member who is breaking a rule.

Host or Hostess. Two Host or Hostess roles are typically assigned; these members model "acceptable social behavior" and serve the refreshments for the group.

Encourager. The Encourager identifies any member who appears to be "left out" or making limited verbal input into the group. He or she attempts to involve that member in the group process or direct the group's attention toward the quiet member.

Role-Player. Two Role-Players may be assigned to carry out any role-play exercises assigned during the session.

Protector. The Protector is allowed to stop any exchange or exercise which may appear to be too difficult or threatening for a particular member. They can ask that a member be excused from the usual group rule that everyone should at least attempt every exercise.

Summarizer. At the end of the session the Summarizer is asked to verbalize, "the main things that went on in this group this session and the main ideas we talked about." The person with this role is also asked to describe one particular thing he or she liked or disliked about the particular session.

Positive Stroker. This member is instructed to "go around the group" at the end of the session and name something positive about each member. This may be a personal characteristic or some behavior which the person demonstrated in the group. In the earlier part of the middle group phases, members may require some assistance from group leaders for this exercise.

Contactor. The group members are divided into two sections, and two Contactors are asked to phone their list of members at least once during the week. They may check on assigned group homework or simply provide support by "checking in" on the other members.

Grader. When homework is assigned, this member, after discussion by the group, assigns a grade for each person's homework.

MORE COMPLEX ROLES WHICH ARE ADDED IN LATER GROUP PHASES

Other Side Viewer. When some issue involves multiple issues that might be viewed from many perspectives, the leader may call on the Other Side Viewer to verbalize another viewpoint opposing one being currently discussed in the group. For example, the member might be asked to verbalize the "parent or adult point of view" or perspective during a discussion of teen responsibility for household chores.

Consequencer. This member is asked to look at the possible consequences of some action or behavior pattern being displayed or discussed in the group. This role allows the group to describe negative consequences of a member's behavior without "preaching."

Inside Voice. This role is modeled after the "alter ego" functioning in psychodrama techniques, where another member stands behind a person in a role-play situation and verbalizes any thoughts and feelings they think the role-player may have which are not being actively verbalized.

Questioner. This member responds in several exercises by asking questions or gaining information about behavior that he or she feels is necessary for the group feedback to others.

Feelings Responder. In some exercises, members rotate the task of responding to and reflecting the feelings they think are being expressed by the member sitting next to them.

Goalmaster. This role is usually assigned to "Peer Mentors," and allows this member to remind other members of their goals, and progress on goals, at any time during the session. Peer mentors are those members who have "graduated" from group after meeting all their goals, but choose to remain in group for more sessions.

GROUP EXERCISES:
MIDDLE TO INTERMEDIATE PHASES

THE NEW LEARNING GAME

The New Learning Game, described earlier, can be used in every phase of group process. At times the therapists may wish to "stack" the cards used in the game. This can insure that cards dealing with specific topics being covered by the group are reflected in the card items. At times when several new members are being introduced into a group, the game serves as a non-threatening introduction to the group for these new members.

GOAL BOOKS

These books are given to each member and contain their original and modified individual goal statements. They also contain space for recorded group feedback on progress by the individual member. The books are also used as the basis for a number of group exercises.

An example of one of the exercises required by the book is to have members verbalize and record their responses to a group exercise labeled, "Forward to the Future." All group members are asked to tell *"Where I would like to be, and what I would like my life to be like 6 years from now."* All members are given a series of homework exercises that involve exploring these goals. Typically, there are a number of goals that are shared by group members (getting a productive job, having their own home or apartment, having their own car, etc.), and group interactions surrounding these issues are normally quite productive.

Another section of the book requires members to verbalize and record *"Things I do, and behaviors I show now, which could keep me from getting where I want to be."* Feedback from other group members and therapists form the basis for a group exercise as the group focuses individually on each member, helping them identify negative behavior patterns. Individualized home-work assignments related to these patterns are given by group leaders.

Below is an example of how these exercises are used in the group. Ruth, an attractive, intelligent 15-year-old whose di-vorced parents continue to compete for her attention and cus-tody, has listed as her 10-year goals: (a) being on my own with a good-paying job that has something to do with creative writ-ing and (b) having a group of friends I like and maybe a special boyfriend.

Group interactions around her verbalized goal statements explored some of her present interests and revealed her to be a sensitive, creative girl who shared brief excerpts from some of her poems and articles for the school newspaper. As homework, she was asked to explore some extensions of her interests as vo-cational goals. Therapists suggested talking with counselors about career possibilities for newspaper work and discussing the realistic limitations on career opportunities for writers. She spontaneously added the task of setting up an appointment to visit a local advertising agency to speak with some of their crea-tive staff.

The extent of her shyness became more apparent when she described the limited number of relationships she attempts, even in the settings she enjoys such as the school newspaper office. The group gave extensive positive feedback about her ability to communicate and interact with them. Following some role-play practice in approaching acquaintances to initiate and sustain a conversation, the group initiated an assignment of homework involving "real" practice at school.

This example shows how effectively the goal statements ap-peared to relate to the book's section, *"Behaviors I show which could keep me from getting where I want to be."* The group also told Ruth, in a supportive fashion, that her "artsy" clothing and make-up style might tend to isolate her from many groups of students at her school before the less tolerant students had an opportunity to learn to like her as a person. Although she ap-peared to have some difficulty accepting this assessment by the group, leaders noted that her clothing became gradually less ec-centric.

The goal books also provide space for "Peer Grading," an evaluation of progress on goals which is completed in interme-diate and end phases of the group.

NEGOTIATION AND POSITIVE
ASSERTIVENESS EXERCISES

Typically several group members bring out problems related to compromising and communicating with others in conflict areas which are similar to experiences of other group members. At this point, leaders initiate some didactic material on basic negotiation and assertiveness skills, review and summarize the basic steps for negotiation, and assign role-play in practice roles. This is followed by group discussion and review of the role-play, focusing on the players' handling of each of the basic steps.

These basic steps are written on large poster board so that members can refer to them in the step-by-step drills of the role-play practice.

1. Know exactly what actions you want from the other person or specifically what you would like him or her to do.
2. Be able to communicate them to the other person in a clear, polite manner.
3. Be able to give clear, adequate reasons *why* you want or need something from the other person.
4. Suggest some solutions to any problems you expect the person might have in doing this for you.
5. Explain and apologize for any misunderstandings or confusion in the past which has kept this person from doing what you are asking of him or her.
6. Offer something to the other person in return for his or her cooperation.
7. Be ready to suggest some compromise or other alternative solution.
8. Express appreciation for any change or compromise from the other person.

Following this drill, those members who have drawn the role-play cards are given a hypothetical conflict situation to role-play and asked to attempt to follow the guidelines in their conflict and negotiation situation. Following the role-play, the entire group continues the drill and practice by giving feedback about whether they thought the players followed each step adequately. ("Did they seem to know exactly what they wanted?" "Could they communicate it well and politely?" "Did they give reasons why they needed something?") Typically group members enjoy this process and other members volunteer to complete other role-play exercises assigned by group leaders. In our structured group, leaders have a repertoire of role-play situations for negotiation, but more typically, the role-plays are suggested by interactions which have been reported by group members from their own environments.

An example of a negotiated conflict solution suggested by a group member is Ralph. He was suspended for 3 days as a result of his perceived involvement in a school cafeteria conflict. He perceived his involvement as attempting to help settle the conflict and felt he had been mistakenly identified as one of the group of actual troublemakers. Following the negotiation steps, Ralph (a) decided to seek a reversal of the suspension decision, which he felt was in error, (b) gathered evidence and witnesses who could explain his actual behavior in the incident, (c) outlined an apology for his ineffective (and very loud) intervention in the incident, (d) outlined in writing an alternative way that he might handle a situation similar to this in the future, where he did not become a part of the problem, but instead became part of the solution, (e) offered to take a survey of students on the complaints about cafeteria food and service system that had led to the current conflicts and "mini-food fight," and (f) called to make an appointment with the principal, and was ready to suggest a partial suspension or in-school suspension as a compromise or alternative solution. As a consequence, the principal, who was very impressed by his positive assertiveness, thorough examination of his evidence and issues, and his creative suggestions for positive solutions, revoked Ralph's suspension. Ralph followed this up with a letter of thanks to the principal which was also signed by his parents.

As a follow-up to this example, when Ralph attempted to negotiate another conflict with a teacher later in the year, he used the same methods with some small success. He reported that some small compromises were reached, but he felt that his expression of thanks for the negotiations were a real factor in changing the teacher's attitude toward him.

"MEMBER HOT SEAT" EXERCISES

At intervals during the group process, each group member will be asked to take the Member Hot Seat. At times members may openly ask for this assignment to have the group focus on an immediate and acute problem area with which they are struggling. A Hot Seat assignment may also be suggested by a Peer Mentor for a specific group member.

The purpose of this exercise is to focus on the needs of a particular member and to encourage the interaction of some more reticent members. The group "goes around" to have each member ask, "something you need to know about what is going on with the Hot Seat Member," and to "share with them any feelings or ideas you have about what they are saying and doing." This gives members formal permission to direct specific questions and encourages intense interactions among members. During this exercise, role-play may be suggested by the leaders and homework assignments may be made which are directly related to issues which were discussed.

As noted earlier, a Member Protector role is either drawn randomly in initial structured role assignments or assigned by the group leaders. The Member Protector may assess the stress level of the Hot Seat Member, deny any specific questions, or simply help the Hot Seat Member to respond or deal with group interactions.

"PARENT HOT SEAT" EXERCISES

At times, members who are dealing with a specific conflict with parents may request that their parents be invited to participate in the Parent Hot Seat exercise. Leaders may also suggest this exercise for a specific member's family. The purpose of the exercise is to (a) provide a protected interchange between member and parents, (b) allow the group and therapists to observe interactions between member and parents, (c) focus on specific conflict areas, and (d) allow practice in negotiation where the group can observe problems in following the basic negotiation steps.

The group prepares for this exercise in the session prior to the hot seat exercise by:

1. outlining the specific problem areas with parent and adolescent;
2. listing a few specific questions for parents which could be possibly approached by negotiating some solutions;
3. assigning a "Group Mouthpiece" role by the random drawing of role tags at the beginning of a session, by group leaders, or by a Peer Mentor who volunteers for this role. The Group Mouthpiece is responsible for read-

ing the questions developed by the group and initiates all activities during the hot seat session;

4. assigning a "Parent Protector." This member's role is to monitor the apparent stress level for the parents. They may disallow any questions that appear too anxiety provoking, and may ask for a redirection of focus if they feel the group interaction has become too stressful around a certain issue;

5. assigning a Member Protector role for each session. This member's role is to monitor stress levels for the adolescent group member whose parents have taken the hot seat role. This person has the same protection functions as the Parent Protector.

Leaders may also assign other roles for this session, including an Other Side Viewer (who may be called upon to give his or her perception of the "other side" to any issue being discussed) and Consequencer (who may be asked to give his or her perception of the consequences of any action being discussed or planned).

To begin the session, the Parent Protector introduces the parents to the group, asks all members to introduce themselves, and identifies himself or herself as the person who can help parents disallow any question they feel is too stressful or personal to pursue in the group. The group is then turned over to the Group Mouthpiece, who introduces the explanation of the purposes of the exercise, explains all roles, and reads the first of the questions which have been previously approved by the group for discussion. The group interchange that follows each question is typically lively and spontaneous, with all members asking and answering questions with the parents.

In addition to questions that are specific to a particular adolescent and parent conflict, the groups have typically added some of the following questions in their pre-session planning: What kinds of things do you like about your adolescent? What are the main things you wish you had done differently with him or her? How can teenagers win back trust from parents once they have lost it? Can they negotiate with you to get more privacy or freedom? What rules do you feel teenagers should have about sexuality and why? How can your teen negotiate with you to make both of you feel better about his or her ideas and behavior in this area?

During the sessions, the parents may also ask any question of the group. The time available during the serving of refreshments has become an opportunity for informal, unstructured contacts between parents and group members, and has become the time when parents have been most spontaneous about bringing up their own questions. Parents have often asked for the group's feedback about their limit-setting. Others have been very effective in using this opportunity to explain their personal reasons for the basis of their rule setting. The intimacy level of the information revealed has often been effective in changing many group members' perceptions of the unreasonableness of their parent's limit-setting. Leaders take notes on the group process and use the information from these sessions to develop the "Issues for Parents" (see Chapter 11).

REFERENCES

Corder, B. F. (in press). *The New Learning Game.*

Corder, B. F., Haizlip, T., & Walker, P. (1980). Critical areas of therapists' functioning in adolescent group psychotherapy: A comparison with self-perception of functioning in adult groups. *Adolescence, 58,* 435-442.

Corder, B. F., Whiteside R., & Haizlip, T. (1981). A study of curative factors in group psychotherapy with adolescents. *International Journal of Group Psychotherapy, 31,* 345-354.

Corder, B. F., Whiteside, R., & Vogel, M. (1977). A therapeutic game for structuring and facilitating group psychotherapy with adolescents. *Adolescence, 46,* 261-268.

10

EXAMPLES OF PROCESS IN VARIOUS PHASES OF A STRUCTURED GROUP

BEGINNING PHASE

Following are excerpts from the 5th session of an outpatient group with six adolescents aged 14 to 16. The group is composed of three females and three males: Allison, Betty, Carole, and Daniel, Eric, and Frank.*

Group rules have already been developed and displayed prominently on a poster in the room. After extinguishing cigarettes in the hall, members file in, continuing the banter they have begun while waiting for group to begin. Everyone chooses their seat and greets the co-therapists. After this exchange, the "role assignment basket" is passed around and each person randomly chooses the badge with the title that will indicate his or her role for the session. Some typical moans and groans ensue, and some members attempt to swap badges until the therapist reminds them of the rule to, "at least try to carry out the role you have chosen."

The Contactor from last week is asked to report on her assignment (calling members to give support, check on homework progress, etc.). Allison reports that she had difficulty reaching

---

*All examples of case material and information used to illustrate group functions are composites of client and case information and do not represent any specific client, group, or verbal exchanges.

Eric and some joking ensues about the double entendre messages she has left with his older brother, who had not been informed about this group procedure.

Carole: Listen . . . I *really* appreciated Allison's calling this week. This was the pits. My best friend Marsha . . . well she used to be my best friend, she had kept me on the phone crying. Her parents are going to put her out of the house if she keeps seeing her boyfriend. They are sure he's dealing dope . . . probably he is. I tried to tell her that, but she doesn't want to hear anything bad about him.

Allison: I told her she can't be responsible for Marsha. Marsha is always begging Carole to do stuff that was the very stuff that got Carole into trouble with her own parents. You can't make your friends keep out of trouble, but she doesn't have to let Marsha get her into it too. Like, if she had gone over there, John could have ended up getting busted. Are the police going to know who is in on all that and who isn't?

[Various nods and brief comments agreeing with this assessment are heard from the group.]

Therapist A: Carole, that is excellent handling of a difficult situation. This is something that you worked on in your homework and really seem to be carrying through. It's hard to know when your responsibility to friends ends, isn't it?

Allison: Well, a real friend should understand that you don't want to get into trouble, and understand when you are scared of getting into *their* trouble. Listen, I wanted to say that next week the Contactor ought to have a list of when you can get calls and when you can't. Frank's mother sounded pissed when I called because it was just after 9:30.

Frank: I'm sorry. My little sister goes to bed at 9:00, and she wakes up if the phone rings. Why don't we pass around a sheet of paper and put on it when the best time to call everybody is.

Betty: Yeah, I got the Contactor badge and I want every one of you to write that down.

Therapist B: Who got the Grader badge? Everybody forgot that you are supposed to be wearing your badge for the whole session so we'll know what you're expected to be doing for the group this session.

Eric: Okay. I got the Grader thing. What do I do . . . go around and make everybody tell if they did their homework?

Therapist B: Yes. And then you get the group to help you give them a grade. The group can make suggestions or disagree with your grade if they had a good reason why. And you give the reason for your grade. Remember about the grade . . . A through F. F means they didn't even try it (homework), and A means they did it perfectly. Then a B if they did most of it real well, a C if they left out an important part, and a D means they didn't try very hard.

Eric: Okay. Then . . . why don't we do Betty . . . we talked a lot about what she was supposed to do about ah . . . about her father and all.

Therapist A: We assigned her to make up a list about her concerns . . . everything she was worried about . . . about having to go visit her father. She has to go visit him, or she thinks she has to. He expects it, about once a month. And she always dreads it. This was one of the things that we said we would do some talking and practice about learning how to negotiate what you want to get.

Betty: Well, I did make up a list, but I wasn't sure that I got what you wanted me to do. *(Pulls list out)* You want me to read it now?

1. When I'm down there . . . at my Dad's, he's always asking me stuff about what's going on at my Mother's . . . you know, if they got a new car, or whatever.
2. Sometimes he talks and talks about how depressed and lonesome he gets . . . like he wants me to say I'm going to come down there and live with him. I don't know what to say to him. What can I say . . . why don't you get a girlfriend or get married or do something so you won't be so lonesome and bored?

Daniel: Yeah, why doesn't he?

Betty: You don't know my father. He mostly complains about everything, and the only people he does anything with are relatives. Every now and then he'll play bridge with them or something.

Therapist A: There's a lot going on in that list, Betty . . . how much you feel responsible, and how much you can really do to help your father . . . and like we were talking about responsibility with friends. How much is he responsible for his own life, and how much can you let him bring you into his own unhappiness and misery? This is something we need to keep talking about and working on.

Eric: Well, we have to give her a grade first, right? We have to grade her homework. Are you finished? *(Betty nods)* Okay, who's got a suggestion? I know what I think. Where's that book . . . didn't you say we were going to put this stuff in a book?

Therapist B: Here it is . . . sorry. I forgot to give you the book. We're going to use these Goal Books the way we talked about. Remember when everybody wrote their goals on the poster over there? This will help us keep up with how well everyone is doing.

Carole: I think she should get an A. She did what you asked her to do (therapists), and she had a good list. Make Frank say . . . he hasn't said a thing yet.

Frank: A.

Carole: *(Laughs)* You can't just say "A." You have to say *why*.

Frank: Well, she said what she thought about her daddy . . . and she brought in the list. What more could she have done?

Group: Yeah. A. *(Eric records an A grade)*

Eric: Allison, you're next. What was your homework?

Allison: *(Sighs)* Well, I was *supposed* to check on whether there was one of those after-school tutoring programs at my school. All I found out is that there is one. I found that out at the office. I have to go back to talk with Mrs. Williams (counselor) this week. It's hard because you have to have something from your teacher or class or something to even go see the counselor and then you have to have something to show you need it (tutoring).

Eric:	Well, did you get it?
Allison:	I didn't have time to do everything.
Daniel:	I thought you said last time the only reason you came to this group was your grades.
Allison:	Give me a break . . . Yeah, it is. But you don't. . . .
Frank:	Listen, she's right. I go to the same school, and it's like, getting permission for anything is like . . . you have to have the president say you can get out of class.
Eric:	Okay. Okay. So what grade do you give her?
Frank:	At least a B . . . she did something on this, but our school . . . it's not easy to do anything there. The teachers are all like Hitler or something. You have to be almost . . . like have a doctor's letter that you have cancer or something to get out of class.

[The group decides to give Allison a "B" for her record after some discussion.]

Therapist A:	You know, one thing I keep thinking is that both Allison and Betty could use some help in negotiating. That is one of the things we said we would talk about in this group, and would practice in this group.
Therapist B:	We have that list. Over here on the poster are all the steps that you have to go through. *(Reads list)*

1. You have to decide what you want.
2. Be able to say it in a clear, polite way, and give the reasons why you want, or need, to have this.
3. Think of the reasons why they wouldn't give it to you before, and have some answers to their objections.
4. Be ready to suggest some compromise or something you could offer them in exchange for their doing what you would like.
5. Be ready to suggest another alternative if the first things you want aren't possible.
6. Thank them politely.

Daniel: I'm the Host. I got the Host badge. And I think we should have the refreshments first. I'm starving.

Therapist A: All right . . . we can be looking over the list while we have Daniel serve the refreshments . . . politely. And everyone will remember to be polite too. Then we'll have Betty and Allison practice some negotiating and do some role-playing of negotiating. Frank, you're wearing the Role-Play badge.

Frank: Yeah. Now what am I supposed to do?

Therapist B: You will be the father with Betty, and maybe the counselor with Allison . . . Betty is going to practice putting some limits on what her father expects. . . .

Betty: I want to stop going down there so often. It's too depressing, and then I get depressed, too.

Allison: Do you have to? I mean is it in the divorce papers that you have to?

Betty: Not really. It says that he has visitation. But it doesn't say I *have* to go down there.

Therapist B: Okay. You can work on that. And Allison, you can work on negotiating some help with your grades. After we have refreshments, we'll do the role-play and let both of you practice some negotiating.

          [The group breaks for refreshments. There are giggles and some kidding around over the exaggerated politeness they use in giving out and accepting the napkins, cups of Coke, and cookies and chips. Some time is spent asking questions and getting clarification about the wording of the negotiation outline poster.]

          [After refreshments, Betty goes over the negotiation steps, lists some of the things she thinks she might be able to get from her father, and goes through the exercise with Frank playing the role of her father.]

Therapist A: Ready Frank and Betty? You know how Betty thinks her father is, Frank? Betty, you can see the steps in negotiating . . . you think you've got it all in mind?

Betty:	I think so. But . . . okay, I'll try it. Couldn't I just do it on the phone?
Carole:	Get real, Betty. You know he wouldn't talk about all that on the phone. You'll just have to face up to this with him.
Frank:	Let's get this show on the road. So you're going down there this weekend. Right? When will you try this?
Betty:	I guess on Saturday. What I'd really like to do is wait till I'm on the way to the plane, but I guess not.
Frank:	What did you want to talk about, Betty?
Betty:	This is really hard to talk about, because I know you are lonesome, and I hate to think of you being lonesome and by yourself. And I don't want you to think that I don't care about you, because I do. And I know you think grandma will think I don't care about you as much as Mom if I don't come here every other weekend.
Frank:	What are you saying? You never want to come here. You just want to stay with your mother and stepfather, and you don't care anything about me, that's it isn't it?
Betty:	That's perfect. He would just pour on the guilt. Just like that.
Frank:	Well, what are you saying?
Betty:	What I would really like to do is, I would like to come once a month instead of every other weekend. It's not because I don't want to see you or anything. It's just that I can't ever really plan stuff that I want to do at school. When there's something good to go to, like a concert comes up, it's on your weekend and I never get to go. And people get tired of asking me to stay over with them, because I'm always going out-of-town. Nobody ever asks me anymore.
Frank:	Well, why didn't you just call me and change your weekend if there is something special you have to do that you want to do?
Betty:	You don't understand. Every other week is just too much to be out of town. I'd be calling you all the time. And I could never really plan ahead for something. And if I did keep calling you and changing the times, I know you would get your

feelings hurt, then I would be upset and it would just end up with everybody getting upset.

Frank: Why don't you just come out and say that you like being with your mother and stepfather and don't like being with me?

Betty: That's not really true. It *is* more fun to be there, because my friends and my school are there, and the things I like to go to, and you know there is nothing going on here that I like to do. You know that.

Frank: Well, it is just a small town. But I would think that you would like to see me too. I *am* your father.

Betty: I know that. And I want to see my father. It isn't that. But I have lots of things I want to do. I can't help it if I don't want to sit around and play cards with grandma every weekend like you do with Aunt Grace and Uncle John. You have to understand that, too.

Frank: I guess I do . . . a little.

Betty: Look, what about this? What if I came one weekend a month, but I wrote you a letter once a week, every week, and I called you on the phone every other weekend? And I would explain everything to grandma, so she would understand that I love you all, but I have lots of things I need . . . that I want to do back at my school, and things to do with my friends. There's hardly anybody here my age. I think she will understand.

Frank: I just don't know.

Betty: Could we just try it . . . just try it for several months and see how it goes? I would talk to grandma and everything. You wouldn't have to do it.

Frank: If that's what you want to do. I'll just be here by myself, thinking about you everyday, and not having anybody to really talk to.

Betty: Boy, that's it, that's it. He would really lay on the guilt.

Therapist B: Go on, Betty, tell him that.

Betty: Daddy, you know I love you and I'm not going to keep on trying to tell you that. You know I do. And if you loved me as much as you say you do, you would want me to be happy, too. Please do

	this for me . . . let me do it and let's see if it won't be okay.
Frank:	I guess we could try it.
Betty:	Thank you, thank you, Daddy. I really appreciate your trying to see my side of it. We will have a better time . . . you'll see. Because I won't mind being here so much, and I can have a better time when I'm here.
Therapist A:	Excellent, you two. Did she follow every one of the steps? Give her some feedback.
Allison:	Betty, it was good. But at first she had trouble saying what she wanted. She was mostly just apologizing or . . . or something.
Daniel:	The best thing was how she came up with that idea of calling him on the phone and writing the letter every week. That was what made him go for it.
Therapist B:	Any other suggestions, ideas?
Betty:	Do you all think he would expect me to do more, or maybe say something about how I don't love my mother any more than him?
Frank:	I don't know. Looks like it wouldn't hurt. But maybe you should wait about saying you would do more to see if he would go for the first part. Are we going to do all this with Allison too?
Eric:	We don't have time to do Allison's role-playing. We haven't gone over all the homework. We have to hear what other people did on their homework.
Therapist A:	Allison, can we do this next time? Can you get all that together to give a good role-play next time? Or if you feel confident about it, you could go on and try it with the counselor at school.
Allison:	I guess I could try it. They're supposed to help me, anyway. That's their job.

[The group goes over homework, grading, and other homework is assigned for next week by therapists. Allison has drawn the Summarizer role, and Carole the Positive Stroker role. The group ends with their functions.]

Allison:	This is hard. Well, everybody did their homework okay except Daniel, and he had a good reason . . .

we let him be excused. Then we went over how you negotiate, and Betty and Frank practiced how she would negotiate with her father to come every month. Then we looked at our goals on the poster, and you (therapists) assigned homework from the goals.

Therapist B: And you are supposed to say what you liked about the group, anything you didn't like, and anything you would like to see us do next time.

Allison: This is hard. I don't want to get this badge next time. Well . . . I like how everybody talked, and we are learning about them. There really wasn't anything I didn't like. And we said we would start with my negotiation role-play next time.

Therapist B: Very good. And summarizing *is* hard to do, Allison. We will help you if you need help. Now Carole has to do the positive strokes. She goes around and stands in front of every member and tells them something she likes about them, or something she likes about the way they did in the group this evening. You have seen us (the therapists) do this before.

Carole: This is embarrassing. Why can't we just sit down and do it? *(She goes and stands in front of each member)* Allison, you did excellent in calling everybody up and you were a big help to me. Betty, you were real good in the role-play and you did everything the chart said. I just hope you can really do that with your father and get what you want. Frank, you were a good role-player. You played her father just like the way Betty said he is. Maybe he wouldn't give in as easy as you did, but you were real good. Daniel, you were our best polite host. And you talked more than you usually do. That was nice that you were not so quiet. Eric, you were a tough grader, but you did good and were real fair.

[The group members acknowledge compliments and positive strokes with embarrassed good nature, and the group leaves with good-natured teasing of Carole.]

MIDDLE PHASE

This section includes excerpts from the 16th session of an outpatient group with six adolescents aged 14 to 16. The group consists of three females and three males: Allison, Betty, Carole, and Daniel, Eric, and Frank.

The group enters promptly with some chatting and a sense of expectation. This is the first session to begin using the "Parent Hot Seat" exercise with its related role assignments. Carole's mother and stepfather have agreed to take the Hot Seat. Prior to this session, the group developed questions that they felt would be useful to ask Carole's parents. In selecting the questions, the group had several goals. Since Carole had complained about her parents' consistently labeling her behavior and actions in a highly negative manner, some positive feedback was requested. Other questions were aimed at giving the parents some group feedback about their limit-setting, and family rules. Carole had described these rules as restrictive and unrealistic.

Therapist A: Okay, Carole's mother and stepfather will be here in about 15 minutes. Is everybody clear about what they're supposed to be doing and the roles that you drew last time? Allison, you're the Group Mouthpiece . . . you have your copy of the questions that the group agreed on?

Allison: Got 'em. Now how much time do I give them to answer this? And what if they won't answer a question?

Therapist B: If they don't want to answer a question, they don't have to. But they have agreed to try it, just as you all agreed when you first came to the group to try some hard things. Daniel, you're the Parent Protector. Feel comfortable about what you're going to do?

Daniel: I watch and see if they look like they . . . something is too hard for them . . . or they act like they can't answer a question. Then I can get the Mouthpiece to ask another question or skip it or something. So the Member Protector. . . .

Eric: I make sure the parents don't get too tough on Carole . . . or if they start giving her a hard time, I can say something.

Daniel: Or change the subject or something.

Frank: And what do I do different this time for the Host?

Therapist A: You bring Mr. and Mrs. C in, and you have everyone introduce themselves. Everybody remember to stand up when the guests come in, please. And the Host will also give out the refreshments as usual.

Carole: Do I get to ask questions too?

Therapist B: Well, you can comment on what they say, just like everybody can . . . and you can ask further questions about their answer. But we have agreed not to bring up a whole question other than the ones we thought were the best ones that the Mouthpiece will ask.

Carole: Do they get to ask questions? Are they supposed to ask just certain questions?

Therapist A: They can ask anything they want. But if we don't want to answer it, we don't have to, and we can say why. And remember that Eric is going to help Carole, and he can say that any question her parents ask her is too hard, or that he thinks it's too hard for her to handle.

Frank: They're here . . . should we go ahead and get started?

[Frank brings in the parents and introduces the members who sit down after parents take their seats.]

Frank: Welcome to the group, Mr. and Mrs. C.

Mr. C: Thank you. We're a little nervous about this whole thing, I have to tell you.

Therapist A: We're a little nervous too, because we want everything to be nice for you all and for Carole, and for good things to come out of this. And to make sure, Daniel is going to help. Tell them, Daniel.

Daniel: I am the Parent Protector, Mr. and Mrs. C. If you feel like some question . . . you don't like it or want to answer it . . . you let me know, or I'll watch too, and you don't have to answer it.

Mrs. C: Thank you . . . that's good to know. We thought about asking you to see the questions in advance. In fact, we asked Carole if we could and she said no.

Therapist B: We hadn't really discussed that in the group. We could have negotiated anything about this meeting. But we have been careful about the questions, and your Parent Protector will help too.

Mr. C: Do we get to ask questions too?

Therapist A: Yes. Whatever you want, and the group will comment on what you say too. We also have a Member Protector, so that if you ask a question that is too hard for Carole . . . tell them about this Eric.

Eric: Well, I get to rule if a question looks too hard for Carole or some other group member. I could mention another question instead.

Allison: Is everybody ready to get started? Okay, first question. "How much privacy do you think a teenager should have, and how much privacy do you give Carole?"

Mrs. C: I think she has plenty of privacy . . . or at least she has privacy . . . I know what she has probably told you . . . she told you about my reading the letter in her room about getting the drugs. She left it out, so when I was cleaning, I read it.

Betty: Excuse me, Mrs. C, but do you think it is right to read somebody's mail?

Mrs. C: Well . . . I wouldn't be reading her mail if we could trust her. We feel we have to check up on her because she has been in so much trouble in the past with drugs, right, John?

Mr. C: You have to earn trust. I'm not saying that Carole was an addict or anything. But she kept pot hidden in her room, and that could get *us* in trouble the same as her. We're not going to have that in our house. Let me ask you people this . . . how much privacy do you have and how can parents know they can trust you?

Betty: My parents never come in my room. They better not. We have a real agreement to respect each other's privacy. But I will have to say, that I have never kept pot in my bedroom. That would make a difference.

Carole: Now, wait a minute. Tell them how long it has been since I had that pot in my bedroom. Tell them how long.

Mrs. C: It has been over a year. But she lied about it to us, and it has made us not trust her. We feel like we have to check up on her. It isn't that we don't want her to have any privacy. Everybody needs privacy.

Therapist A: So you are saying that you would like to give her the privacy she wants . . . to keep her bedroom only to herself, and her letters to herself. But you have worries. . . .

Mr. C: That's right. We don't feel like we can trust her after we found the pot. And she used to go around with some of the kids they called druggies at school. One of them was even arrested.

Allison: Mr. C, haven't you seen a change in Carole, though? In the group she has talked about lots of times she had a chance to get in trouble . . . she was invited to get into trouble and she didn't do it. She even has stayed away from some of her friends that are really going to get in trouble because she knows she could get involved.

Mrs. C: We have seen some changes in her. I would be the first to say that. She seems like she's more like the old Carole that she used to be. And she was the sweetest little girl that you have ever seen.

Carole: Oh, my God, Mother.

Mrs. C: She was. And she is still a sweet and loving girl. A lot of her behavior . . . she is just acting tough.

Allison: This is getting into one of our other questions, Mrs. C. The question was, "What do you think are the good things about Carole?"

Mr. C: Carole has plenty of sense. And she can be a pleasure to be around when she wants to be.

Mrs. C: Oh, my. She is pretty and smart, and very loving. We all love her. I guess that's one of the reasons . . . I just get so scared of . . . we could lose her. It just scares me to death that we could lose her.

Carole: What do you mean?

Mrs. C: I mean, something *could* happen to you from drugs . . . but I think that, really, I'm not worried about that now. I don't say much about this, but Carole's father . . . he doesn't do much for her, and they are not very close. But he always blames me for any problem she has. He has threatened me

	before. If she gets in trouble, real trouble . . . he is going to sue me for custody and he has enough influence that he might be able to do it.
Carole:	You never said that to me, did you? I never knew that you were worried about that.
Mrs. C:	I think about it all the time. I worry about it all the time. It would kill me to lose you. *(Mrs. C appears near tears; Carole comes over and hugs her)*
Therapist B:	Maybe that explains to Carole some of the reasons you seem to be so strict on her sometimes.
Mrs. C:	It is one of the big reasons. She is my baby.
Therapist B:	Carole, I think your mother is saying some important things to you.
Carole:	Yeah, I really didn't know she was so worried about that happening.
Therapist B:	Maybe you'd like to just sit there by your mother. *(Carole pushes her chair over to her mother)*
Allison:	Daniel, you're the Parent Protector . . . can we go on to the next question.
Daniel:	Yes, I think so.
Allison:	It's about the same thing, really. "Could you and Carole practice negotiating some rules in here that could satisfy you both about the privacy and some other rules?"
Therapist A:	By that we mean, try to get some rules that would settle some of your fears about losing Carole. What were some of your other concerns, Carole?
Carole:	Oh, yeah. I wanted to stay out later on the weekends. I have to be in at 10:00 and the movies don't even get over by then.
Therapist A:	Okay. Let's negotiate one thing at a time, Carole. Let's start with the privacy. There are the rules over there Mr. and Mrs. C. The rules for negotiating. *(Points to chart)* Carole has had some practice. So we'll let her start.
Carole:	What I would like is to not have you go in my room, Mother, and look through my things and read my mail. It makes me feel like . . . like no part of the whole house is mine or my own. And it has been a year since I had pot in the house . . . I won't say I have never smoked one joint since that time . . . but it has been almost *nothing*, and I have *never* brought anything home since then. Okay.

	(Looks at chart) Look, if I make a promise that I will never have anything like that in the room, will you promise not to go all through it? And if you know I am not smoking any pot at all?
Mr. C:	Wait, Carole, how do we know you will keep your promise?
Carole:	It's been a year since that happened, alright? And you can ask the people in here. I've really tried to keep from being around George and anybody who's into drugs. You just don't know how much stuff I have stayed away from. The only thing I know is, you have to trust me, and if I break that trust, you would do what you think you have to do. Besides, you know I would never want to live with my Dad.
Mrs. C:	I would be willing to try it. I think I could tell if you had been smoking pot. And I would be willing not to go in your room, if I could be absolutely sure you weren't using any drugs. That would mean you're not keeping up your part of the bargain. Your part of the bargain would have to be that you're not smoking pot in or out of the house.
Carole:	That's no big deal. I practically never do anyway. I can promise that. Now how about the curfew? Anybody knows that 10:00 is too early, because you can't even get back from the movie by that time. If you let me stay out till 11:00, I would promise not to go around George. And I would call you to let you know where I am, say at 9:00, if I decided not to go to the movie. You always complain if I make even one little change from what I told you we'd be doing.
Mr. C:	Well, yes. Because we are responsible for you and you could be off dead somewhere and we wouldn't even know where you are because we thought you were at the movie.
Carole:	Okay, okay. I promise to call and let you know any change and let you know where I'll be. Will you be willing to just try it? You could always change back if I don't keep my word.
Mrs. C:	I guess we would be willing to try it. For a month, do you think so, John?

Mr. C:	We've always been willing to try different things. We just haven't been able to count on Carole to keep her end of the bargain.
Therapist A:	It looks like a lot of the privileges and things that you have wanted to get are up to you now, Carole. To do what you promised, so you can be trusted.
Carole:	Yeah. I can handle it.
Therapist A:	Mr. and Mrs. C, we promised you would not have to be on the Hot Seat too long. Do you have time to answer a few more questions from the group, or do you have questions you'd like to ask them?
Mr. C:	They can ask us some questions if they want to.
Frank:	I have two questions: Do you think Carole has changed since she has been in the group? And are you folks ready for a Coke?
Mr. C:	Yes and yes.
Mrs. C:	Carole is a lot easier to talk to since she's been in this group. And she seems to be around a lot nicer friends. She even seems to dress differently. I think she just gets prettier all the time.
Carole:	Oh, God, Mother.
Therapist A:	Sometimes Carole has trouble accepting compliments, but she really likes them, Mrs. C. How about our break now, while Frank gets our refreshments?

[After refreshments are served, the group stands, shakes hands with parents, the Host and Mouthpiece thank them for coming, and Carole accompanies them to the door, her arm around her mother, returning for the group summary and discussion of the session.]

Carole:	What a trip! I can't believe my mother. She never told me the reason she was so strict was she was afraid of losing me.
Eric:	Afraid of losing her baby.
Carole:	Oh, shut up.
Allison:	I think that was sweet. It shows how much Carole means to her.
Therapist B:	It does seem as if Carole's mother really cares a lot about her and worries about losing her. But it also seems that she has to be sure that Carole isn't go-

ing back to smoking pot again before she can completely trust her. What did you all think about the negotiating?

Carole: I didn't do it all in order, but I can't believe they agreed to everything.

Therapist B: But you have a lot of responsibility too.

Carole: Yeah. I know.

Therapist A: Everything that is a change takes work, and you will have to make sure that you keep your part of the bargain, Carole. That's something we need to talk more about. But we just have time for a quick summary now. Everybody else had another role for this session, so Dr. W and I will do the summary.

Therapist B: I was so impressed with the way your mother showed how much she cared for you, and how that was part of the reason she was strict with you. And the other part seemed to be that you had been involved with some folks who were into drugs, Carole. Staying away from them as a part of your negotiating seemed smart. Your stepfather seemed to be pretty reasonable too. And I was proud of the group. You were all really grown up and mature and helped make this session a good one.

Betty: You're doing my part! I'm the Positive Stroker for this session.

Therapist A: Right. Let's hear some good stuff about this group.

Betty: Allison was a good Mouthpiece. She knew when to break in and ask the question, and was polite. Frank did a good job as the Host . . . serving the refreshments and making them comfortable. Eric and Daniel were good Protectors. I don't think things got . . . uncomfortable, do you? And Mr. and Mrs. C felt the same way, because they said so when we were having refreshments. They said they were worried about it at first, but that it wasn't bad at all.

Therapist B: Excellent, Betty. You always give good feedback to everybody. Frank, you're the Contactor for next week? We'll see you all next week.

LATER PHASE

This section includes excerpts from the 28th session of an outpatient group with six adolescents aged 14 to 16. The group consists of three males and three females: Allison, Betty, Carole, and Daniel, Eric, and Frank.

A brief review of one of the structured role assignment exercises will be helpful in following selected excerpts from this session. These excerpts offer examples of one of the more difficult structuring techniques used in the group. We go around the group asking each member to report on his or her week and to share with the group any feelings or experiences that are important. Three special roles are assigned to allow the group to take responsibility for the therapeutic work of the group. As each member speaks or makes some input into the group, the member on his or her left takes the role of "Feelings Responder." That member must respond with some statement about the feelings that he or she feels are expressed by the speaker. He or she must also add some information about his or her own feeling response to statements made by the speaker. The member on the right of the speaker becomes the "Questioner." His or her function is to ask any further questions which he or she feels the group may need to know to understand what is going on with the present speaker.

The third role is normally given to members as an honor, or when they become "Peer Mentors" after having reached all their initial goals for group membership. The "Goalmaster" may relate any statement at any time to a member's current goals.

In this session Eric is Goalmaster. He has met his stated goals of improving his grades, negotiating a "truce" with his parents on conflicts about grades, and negotiated new house rules for curfew, driving the family car, and so on. Betty speaks first. Daniel, on her left, becomes the Feelings Responder. Allison, on her right, becomes the Questioner for the group.

Betty: Well, I almost wasn't here tonight . . . my Dad did it again. Messed up my entire weekend. I thought things were a lot better . . . they are in a way, since we got this agreement about my not going down there but once a month or every other month . . . but then he always picks the time and at the last minute, he has this overtime he has to do, and then he wants to change the weekend.

Daniel: It looks like you should be happy. You didn't want to go anyway, but you just act miserable and angry. I feel like you'd maybe rather be miserable than do something about it.

Betty: Of course, I'm angry! I could have done something with my friend, but she thought I would be at my Dad's so she went out-of-town. So there I sat by myself all weekend with nothing to do. And this is the second time he's done it. I *am* glad I didn't have to go . . . but. . . .

Allison: You just let him do it. Did you feel like you couldn't say anything? You took up for yourself before, when you worked out not going down there every other weekend. You even got up to every other month sometimes. What keeps you from just telling him?

Betty: I don't know. I just couldn't. I just said okay. *(Moans from other group members)*

Eric: Betty, you have done one thing you want to do . . . you got out of going down to see your Dad every other weekend. But you never really told him how you *felt* about any of it. You just gave all these reasons why . . . good reasons why you needed to be here more on the weekend, and why you wanted to be here. But did you really say how you felt?

Betty: No, I didn't. I know we did some of it here (role-playing), but I know I couldn't do it down there, and I couldn't do it over the phone . . . that seems so. . . .

Eric: Okay. How about a letter . . . why can't you write him some of your feelings in a letter?

Daniel: Yeah! You're good at writing. That poem you read was really good.

Betty: Maybe I could. I could do that better than saying it over the phone.

Eric: We could all help you with it . . . we could write the letter here in the group.

Betty: You could help me with it, you could . . . make changes after I get it done . . . let me do it and I'll bring it in next time.

Therapist A: Betty, would you like to write two letters . . . the one you're really going to mail and one that you

	probably wouldn't mail, but says a lot of things you need to say?
Eric:	Yeah! Betty, it's time for you to let your Dad know how you feel about some things.
Betty:	I know it. You're right.
Daniel:	But you dread it because he's going to be hurt and maybe cry like that time . . . and you think you're gonna be feeling worse . . . even than if you did whatever he wants.
Betty:	Uh-huh. But let me bring the letter next time.
Frank:	If we're going to help Betty write a letter to her Dad, how about helping me write one to Paula.
Carole:	I'm your Questioner, right? I thought we decided you could never tell how she felt about you, and she never let you know her true feelings. So you never knew where you stood with her. Didn't you tell everybody you were going to give up on her? So what's the deal here?
Allison:	Dr. C is sitting there, so that makes me your Feelings Responder. Well, doesn't that piss you off a little at Carole? It does me. Because you finally found somebody that . . . a girlfriend. Just because you don't know right away how she feels about you, that doesn't mean you should give up . . . maybe she doesn't even know herself how she feels.
Eric:	Yeah, that was one of your goals.
Frank:	Carole didn't mean anything by. . . .
Carole:	No, I wasn't trying to push you. I'm just that way. I just tell somebody straight out, just where . . . just what I think. I'm direct.
Eric:	And speaking of goals . . . being that way, that was one of the things that just about got you punched out in the girl's bathroom at school. And one of your goals . . . you said you wanted to get along better.
Carole:	I apologize, Frank. Start over. I'm working on that, I really am *(laughs)*.

This brief excerpt gives some flavor of the effects of the rotating role assignments of Questioner and Feelings Responder. In our group experience, these structured role assignments have not impeded the spontaneous flow of interchange among group members. Instead, the roles have seemed to result in an increase in members' taking responsibility for the process and depending less on interventions from the therapists.

11

ISSUES FOR PARENTS*

GENERAL SUGGESTIONS

POSITIVE FEEDBACK

Sometimes it is hard to remember, but adolescents need to hear good stuff about themselves as well as hearing about the things they need to improve. How about some "good talk" fairly often that emphasizes the positive things about your adolescent?

PRIVACY

Adolescents need their privacy, and it is very important to them. Here are some of the specific areas about which the group has suggested making family rules.

Privacy in Their Rooms. This is the adolescent's private domain and should be treated as such, as long as he or she follows family rules of behavior for using that room. Some of the typical family rules are: no storing or use of illegal substances, no smoking (if that is a family rule), and no hiding of items tak-

---

*Adapted from "Suggestions for Parents From the Booklet." This booklet was developed by Dr. Billie Corder and Dr. Reid Whiteside from their work with several groups. For more information about this, please contact Dr. Corder.

en from other family members. Privacy means that parents will not come into the adolescent's room without knocking, will not search his or her clothing or furniture, and will not make changes in the room without permission. In turn, the adolescent must agree to keep the room at least nominally clean, remove his or her own linen and clothing for laundry, and return them to storage in the room.

The group has talked about the ways that adolescents can lose some of their rights to privacy. These include (a) keeping drugs or other substances in their room, (b) indicating that they might make some plans to hurt themselves, and (c) leaving some "incriminating evidence" around, as if they want you to see it (such as letters to friends planning a pot smoking party).

Once adolescents have lost their privacy rights, they need to know what it takes to get their privacy rights back again. The following examples of room privacy include suggestions for negotiating the return of privacy rights after they have had to be taken away.

Privacy as it Relates to Self-Destructive Behavior, Threats, or Statements. If they have made any threats to hurt themselves: (a) They might discuss this with parents in therapy. (b) They might expect and allow regular checks on them when they are in their rooms alone. (c) They might discuss this with very close friends, who must be allowed (given verbal permission) by the group member to contact parents and therapists if the group member makes other self-destructive threats or statements. (d) They might have all medications, guns, and other items which could be used to harm themselves taken from the house or locked up. (e) They might come up with some constructive suggestions for things they would like to work on changing in their life, their family, and themselves. This way the positive changes can be worked on in therapy and at home. (f) They might have parents and therapists work together to help the group member negotiate the amount of time necessary before the adolescent can return to the old rules of privacy.

Privacy as it Relates to Taking Things from Others and Hiding Them in Their Room. Adolescents may temporarily lose their right to privacy in their room (a) when they have taken something from others and hidden it in their room and (b) when parents have had to check their belongings for stolen items because there has been enough evidence in the past that they have taken items from family members or others.

The return to old rules for privacy can be negotiated by setting a period of time for "restitution" and setting up some time period during which the adolescent shows he or she will not repeat the behavior. For example, restitution could involve doing special things for the person whose belongings have been taken, or having his or her allowance taken away for a period of time to pay for the stolen item. Set a reasonable time period, depending on the value of the item taken or the distress it caused the person from whom it was taken (at least a month for an item valued by another person). Then return to the old rules for privacy.

Privacy in Telephone Conversations. The telephone and privacy for using it is a valuable and treasured item for adolescents. They should be allowed to make and receive phone calls as often as possible, in as much privacy as possible, when they prove they can be responsible.

Responsibility means that they are considerate in ways such as: (a) They do not receive phone calls after family bedtimes when the phone might disturb others. (b) They do not monopolize the phone and keep other family members from making or receiving calls. (c) They do not run up long-distance phone bills they cannot pay themselves. (d) They do not use the phone for conversations involving plans for self-destruction or involvement in illegal activities.

Telephone privileges should be removed temporarily if adolescents do not live up to their responsibilities. The length of time teens should be restricted from using the telephone should be negotiated between parent and teen, but probably should not exceed 1 week. After that time, a new "trial of responsibility" should be set.

If rules continue to be broken, the restriction time may need to be increased before a new trial of responsibility is given.

Privacy in Written Correspondence. All correspondence to and from the adolescent should be given complete privacy. This means that it is not read by parents and family. This privilege can be lost when the adolescent has written plans for self-destructive or illegal behavior in correspondence or has "accidentally" left letters or notes around in other areas of the home whose contents cause unusual concern to parents (plans for breaking serious rules, illegal or self-destructive behavior, etc.).

Privileges can be regained after parents and adolescent negotiate some solution to the behavior which is the basis for these concerns. Therapists may have to help with this.

"FREEDOM" OR INDEPENDENCE FOR THE ADOLESCENT

Most teens want all the independence they can get. The group has discussed what is probably realistic in terms of the amount of independence most parents are comfortable with, and the amount a teen can usually handle. Some areas of independence and methods for negotiating rules and regulations which have been suggested by the group are curfew and time limits.

Curfew and Time Limits. Each family has its own needs and framework for curfew, based on everyone's need for rest and ability to handle their work or school loads. This has to be negotiated with individual teens and their parents. The important thing seems to be to allow teens to *try* their own suggested limits on curfew, to see if they can handle it by obeying the limits completely while continuing to handle their work and school load and remaining healthy and alert. However, the other members of the family and their needs must be taken into consideration.

If curfew or time rules are broken, a specific time should be set to allow the teen to be grounded or make some restitution (be given extra chores, etc.). The length of time should depend on the anxiety caused for other members of the family by the rule breaking or the general seriousness of the rule breaking (how long they were gone, whether or not it was avoidable, etc.). Generally a short (no more than a week) grounding or punishment works best for less serious offenses. Restitution may also be expected (no allowance, extra chores, etc.).

GENERAL RULES ABOUT SEXUAL BEHAVIOR

Each family has to negotiate its own rules and expectations about sexuality, based on the family's beliefs, religion, and so forth. Generally, adolescents will each have to work out their own moral values, and when they are alone, they will have to make their own judgments and decisions, and decide what is responsible behavior.

Parents should make very clear what they think is acceptable behavior and tell adolescents what they expect from them. This does not mean that adolescents will be able to accept the parents' values or standards.

Parents should, if possible, let adolescents know that they do not find certain behaviors acceptable, and do not condone them. If the parents feel they are able to do this, they may add that they will not take their love away if these rules are broken. They may be disappointed, concerned, and upset, but should not hate the adolescents for their different sexual standards.

In turn, adolescents should not always expect parents to have the same ideas and standards. They should respect the reasons for their parents' standards as well as show respect for their parents' feelings. They should not expect parents to allow or condone behavior which is unacceptable to their parents' standards and should not flaunt such behavior in front of their parents.

Many adolescents will use their own standards for handling sexual behavior. These standards may be different from their parents'. If parents do not agree, they may have difficulty discussing birth control options, or they may not believe in allowing these options. The group feels that if people are going to be sexually active, they should have protection to avoid pregnancy and to avoid sexually transmitted diseases. The group suggests that parents make it clear that they do not condone any standards different from their own, but *do not actively interfere with the adolescents' seeking out some information and help in birth control planning and protection from sexually transmitted diseases.* Parents can do this by telling their teens their own standards but allowing them to take responsibility for their own behavior.

In turn, teens should not expect parents to assume the responsibility for taking care of any children they may have. If they are old enough to be sexually active, they are old enough to plan birth control responsibly or make tough and sad decisions about how they must handle an unwanted pregnancy, forced marriage, or difficult single parenting.

SUBSTANCE ABUSE AND HANDLING THIS IN THE HOME

Parents have certain legal responsibilities as well as their own standards for handling alcohol, pot, and other substance abuse. Legally they may not allow or condone this use by minors. Privileges and allowances may be removed for minor offenses. Therapy and perhaps inpatient help in specialized facilities may be sought if teens demonstrate a real abuse problem. Many teenagers today indicate that they have experimented with alcohol or other substances. Parents should express their attitudes and rules, and are expected to punish even minor offenses. Consequences may be negotiated between teen and parent.

GRADES AND SCHOOL WORK

All parents want their teen to achieve well in school. Each person's problem with achievement is different. Sometimes a therapist is needed to negotiate the expectations and rules for study, grades, and so on. Most adolescents agree that certain hours for daily studying can be set. Some teens in the group feel that they might need some special tutoring or help to "catch up," but this is seldom effective when given by a parent and usually leads to conflicts. Essentially the group felt that some restriction on dating or activities during school days was helpful. They felt that most punishment or extensive grounding was not usually helpful in bringing up grades. If the reason for bad grades is a poor academic background, some remedial help is needed. If the reasons are emotional, some therapy which will help negotiate changes and set realistic goals is probably needed. In general, the group felt that parents cannot "force good grades by punishment."

12

A SPECIALIZED SHORT-TERM
STRUCTURED THERAPY GROUP
FOR SEXUALLY ABUSED
YOUNG ADOLESCENT GIRLS

Although there is some controversy over reliability of available data, many researchers feel that the number of females in our society who have been victims of some type of sexual abuse may conservatively be estimated as one out of every five (Burgess et al., 1978). If these predictions are accurate, the need for education and therapeutic interventions that are effective and cost-efficient may be overwhelming. In addition, there is some indication that traditional psychotherapy with traumatized children may fail to alleviate some of the initial symptoms of anxiety. Terr (1981) in her study of children involved in the Chowchilla school bus kidnapping, reported that these children continued to display reenactment of the event and other symptoms of anxiety even after therapeutic intervention. In our current work, we have concluded that techniques that specifically structure opportunities for the mastery of the traumatic experience should probably be the primary focus of the therapy (particularly in relatively brief interventions), rather than focusing more extensively on cathartic explorations of reactions to the experience. In addition, liaison work with Michael Rutter (1978), and the research of Anthony and Cohler (1987), has indicated some concepts in the development of defense mechanisms of "invulnerable children" who cope successfully with chronic stress and trauma which may be useful in treatment of sexual abuse.

The coping mechanisms of these invulnerable children have been described as cognitive relabeling of the environment, the ability to attract and seek help from others in the environment, good problem-solving ability, intellectualization, and the capacity for maintaining self-esteem. Our own research has focused on the possibility of structuring therapy to develop these mechanisms with sexually abused children, in order to foster their mastery of this trauma (Corder, DeBoer, & Haizlip, 1990; Corder & Haizlip, 1989).

Our groups have been held with young adolescent girls, aged 12 to 13, who were referred to us by a county department of social services following substantiation of sexual abuse. These girls had received a limited amount of individual intervention from staff of the department of social services. The girls were within the average range of intelligence, and their families were within the upper-lower to lower-middle socioeconomic levels.

STRUCTURED TECHNIQUES AND
MATERIALS USED IN THE GROUPS

The structured materials used in the groups were developed over a 2-year period of working with other sexually abused children in individual sessions. These materials were used to structure the sessions for the groups within a 20-week, time-limited, closed-membership group. Sessions lasted 1 hour. Mothers who ranged in age from 25 to 34, were invited to attend every third session of the group, after the initial session.

SESSIONS ONE THROUGH THREE

Session One. In the first session, the girls are randomly paired with each other for a brief period during which they are asked to find out some information about each other which they would use to introduce their partners to the group. The information includes giving their partner's name, age, school, three special interests, and at least one thing they would like to achieve in this group. At the same time, mothers are paired with each other and given a similar task. Information shared by mothers includes name, number of children, work outside the home, and what they would like to see happen in this group.

The group leaders outline the goals of the group as: learning they were not alone in their experiences, being able to express their feelings about the sexual abuse, learning to feel good about themselves and their ability to deal with both the abuse and other problems in their lives, learning ways to recognize and stop any future abuse attempts, learning the facts about sexual abuse (understanding the causes, what is known about treatment, etc.), and understanding and working on the feelings between mothers and daughters surrounding sexual abuse by a father or father substitute.

The group leaders describe a "Getting Safe and Strong Book" that the group will write together, using information and discussions from the group, for each member to keep as a reminder of our work.

Sessions Two and Three. The second and third sessions are used to build relationships and establish group goals to which the participants can be committed. The leaders go around the group, asking each girl to name "three wishes" about sexual abuse. The leaders set the stage by noting "We can't make these wishes come true, but we will work together on each wish as much as we can in the group. We will talk about ways to handle our feelings about the wishes that cannot be made to come true, and find what parts of the wishes we can make happen."

Many of the girls express similar "wishes," but the following list covers the range of their concerns. They are listed in order of the perceived importance by the group.

We wish that:

1. the abuse never had happened.
2. the sexual abuse had not been by someone like a parent or stepparent that we liked and trusted in some ways.
3. it would never happen again.
4. it would never happen to our sisters or brothers . . . or to anyone.
5. the abuse had not been more than once.
6. we could just forget about it.
7. the person who did it would not deny it.
8. our mother and everyone had believed us from the beginning.
9. we would be able to understand why someone would do this to us.

10. we had known not to trust some people, and known whom we could trust.
11. we could have been able to have sex for the first time with someone we really loved.
12. the person who did it could be cured.
13. if they could be cured, that our family could be back together again.

When mothers attend the next session, the girls' wishes are shared with them, and the mothers are asked to share some wishes of their own. These wishes are listed below.

We mothers wish that:

1. our family had not been so affected.
2. we could stop loving the person who abused our child, and not have any more positive, confusing feelings toward them.
3. our daughters could understand why we had trouble believing them at first.
4. our daughters could make a special effort to comply with rules and not have conflict during this difficult period.

Listing each of these "wishes" elicits extended discussion in the groups. Along with a cathartic exploration of feelings, the discussion brings out a number of issues related to the abuse.

One of the purposes of the "listing" is to develop the specific goals of the group and to have the goals relate directly to the needs of the members. After the wishes are written on a blackboard or large poster board, leaders review the list and use it to structure goals. The restated "goals and wishes" list usually reads like the following.

In this group:

1. we will learn to handle feelings and fears about the sexual abuse.
2. we will learn that we can have two opposite feelings about the same people, and that people who have many good things about them can also have a sick, opposite side which lets them be abusers, and makes us unable to trust them.

3. we can definitely learn to make ourselves safer and avoid being victims again. We can learn ways to protect ourselves.

4. we can learn ways to teach our sisters and brothers to protect themselves and keep themselves safe.

5. we can learn the reasons from each other that we were afraid to tell about the abuse or were afraid to try to stop the abuse at that time. *That was then and this is now. Now* we will learn how to get help immediately.

6. we cannot forget about it completely, but we will learn ways of "thought stopping," and how to change the ways that we think to ourselves about the abuse.

7. we may not be able to get the person to confess, but we can understand better why they did it and why they can't admit it. And we will practice what we would really like to say to them about it.

8. we will learn all the reasons why a mother has problems accepting that something this frightening can happen right in her own family, and why she may have tried to keep this from her own knowledge because of the fear and anger this could cause a mother.

9. nobody knows *exactly* what causes sexual abuse, but we will talk about the reasons some people believe it happens and we will understand it better. This will help us not to be a victim again and understand that anyone could be abused if they were not *taught* how to protect themselves.

10. unless they are taught before the abuse happens and understand all the things we are learning now, it is hard to know whom to trust when we are so young. But there are situations that we will learn to avoid, and what to do when they happen.

11. we will learn sexual abuse is not the same as loving sex. It is harmful to the abused person. We can have loving sex, a very different thing, when we are older and ready to love someone emotionally and physically. This is something we will talk about and understand.

12. we will talk about the methods that are used to help some people who sexually abuse others. But people have to be willing to get help, and those who are not willing are not likely to change.

13. we will talk about all the wishes for our family, and which ones seem more realistic. If families are not able

to get back together, we will talk about what that will mean. If some of our families are going to try to live together again, we will talk about how to keep safe in that situation.

The mothers' "wishes" in this instance were restated into the following goals.

In this group:

1. we will learn the ways that the family is usually affected, handle some of these feelings in the group, and talk about the ways that these feelings can be handled at home.
2. we will learn that we can have opposite feelings about the same person, and look at what we can realistically expect from people who have lost our trust.
3. one of the goals for our girls is to have them understand the problems a parent has in believing something very frightening and negative which has been happening within their own family. Mothers will also learn why this was so difficult and frightening for them.
4. we can try to understand all the reasons that there is conflict and anger within a family where there has been sexual abuse, and we will work on handling those feelings within the group and at home.

SESSIONS FOUR AND FIVE

The group members are asked to list the three "Band-Aids" they need for the most difficult hurts which had resulted from the abuse. Again the "Band-Aids" are listed on a blackboard or poster board. The girls in this instance listed the following as their major concerns, in order of perceived importance.

The things that hurt me that
I need a "Band-Aid" for are:

1. the way things changed with my mother, and my mother not believing me.
2. having to deal with angry feelings toward my mother, as well as angry feelings toward the abuser.

3. wondering why my mother didn't realize what was going on and do something about it.
4. losing my father (or stepfather, or father substitute), or someone the rest of the family needed in some ways.
5. feeling blamed and feeling left out of good things by other family members after the abuse was made known.
6. feeling that I was different, and that other people could tell in some way what had happened to me.
7. feeling that I didn't really understand anything about what was going on.

In a related session attended by mothers, these lists of hurts were reviewed, and mothers were encouraged to make their own list which was as follows.

Mothers need a "Band-Aid" for:

1. feeling betrayed by our husband or boyfriend (the abuser).
2. feeling confused about our need for support and for having a husband, and our anger and disgust over his behavior.
3. feeling that our daughters were becoming more difficult to discipline, just when we have so many problems with finances, and have to handle our own confused, angry feelings.
4. feeling criticized by social services and other family members for not being more protective of our daughters.

Again these "hurts" were restated in the form of goals for the group which were focused on mother-daughter shared understanding of the reasons for the abuse, mothers' difficulty in understanding and accepting what had happened, and plans for exercises which could help mothers and daughters express their feelings and negotiate compromises in behavior expectations, chores, and so on.

In these sessions, a surprising number of mothers have revealed that they were sexually abused by father figures or other family members in their own childhood. This typically comes as a shock to their daughters, who react with disbelief, compassion, and some anger because, "You should have known it could happen again." Most of the members are able to accept that this experience might make a mother even more confused and unable to accept that abuse had been repeated with her daughter. One of the goals for the group members that usually results from this type of discussion is to develop skills for telling their own daughters about sexual abuse and protecting themselves so that this pattern will not be repeated in the next generation.

SESSIONS SIX THROUGH EIGHTEEN

These sessions use structured exercises and techniques to direct the discussion and interpersonal exchanges related to the specific goals outlined previously. Some didactic material on the prevalence of sexual abuse is introduced by leaders for group discussion. The girls are allowed to read over some of the booklets which have been developed for younger children by the therapists. This serves a number of purposes. Girls who are less verbal see the material presented on a more simple level, and they are able to use some of the material to structure the things they wanted to tell their younger sibling about protecting themselves from abuse.

SOME ADDITIONAL IDEAS

THE "WOULDN'T IT BE NICE" BOOKLETS

Designed primarily for use by younger children, these booklets are in the form of coloring books to be used as a discussion guide in structured groups for children aged 6 through 9. The pages are laid out in pairs with the same format. As pages are opened, the left side of the book is divided into two parts: The top half of the page has illustrations to be colored that depict some wishes and myths which have been expressed by abused children. One example is: "Wouldn't it be nice if . . . you were very, very good, then nothing bad would ever happen to you." This is illustrated by a little girl with a halo above her head, looking very angelic. The bottom half of the page shows an illustration to be colored and discussed. It is labeled, "But the way it *really* is. . . ." In the preceding example, this bottom half explains, "Even if you are very, very good, this does not keep bad things from happening to good people sometime. Good people can get sick with illness, good people can have accidents, and good people can be sexually abused. When bad things happen, it does not mean that you are being punished for being bad."

The full page facing these divided pages is labeled "What We Can Do About It." It is illustrated with pictures to color and contains information about how to handle typical problems. The group discusses and practices problem-solving skills, and works on mastery development exercises which are described on these pages.

In the example given, the "What We Can Do About It" page lists (a) going to groups like this one to understand that sexual abuse can happen to anyone before they know how to protect themselves, (b) you can understand that you were not chosen to be abused because you were bad, but usually because you were available to the abuser, and (c) you can learn ways to talk to yourself about these feelings in this group.

COGNITIVE RELABELING OF THE EXPERIENCE AND DEVELOPMENT OF SELF-ESTEEM

In each session there is time for going around the group for structured positive feedback to increase self-esteem. This is similar to the "brags" used by Berliner and Ernst (1984) in their work. At the session's end, each girl is asked to say "something good about the way each person in the group participated today," and the group leaders add individual "verbal positive strokes" for each member.

As part of the cognitive relabeling of their abuse experiences, as well as techniques for "thought stopping," the girls are taught a number of "chants" and "cheers." They rehearse these in the group and are asked to repeat them to themselves when they feel under stress. Examples include:

> "I'm a good person, I'm proud of me. I've been through a lot, but look how strong I've got."

> "That was then, but this is now. I *won't* be abused, and I know *how*!"

THE MOVING ON AND GETTING STRONGER GAME

Two versions of this original board game are used depending on the group (preadolescent and adolescent). The game is geared toward a positive relabeling of their mastery of the abuse experiences. The game board shows children progressing from Sad Valley, to Mixed-Up Mountain onward to Learning Lake, Positive Prairie, and finally ending at Safe Plain and Smart Mountain, as they learn mastery skills. They roll dice to select the number of places to move around the board. The places are labeled to correspond with stacks of "Learning Cards," "Practicing Cards," or "Telling Cards."

The Learning Cards require players to answer factual questions about some of the didactic material being covered in the group. (*Example*: Ask somebody in the group to estimate how many children in this city have been sexually abused. Have the group leaders tell whether they think this answer is right or wrong.)

The Practicing Cards require players to role-play a situation described on the card. The group member has to find an adequate solution to the problem situation described. (*Example*: A person in your church, who has made you feel funny or scared in the past, asks your mother if he can take you to the park on a picnic. What would you say to your mother and what would you do?)

Telling Cards require the group member to share something personal about the sexual abuse experience, or about their reaction to it. These items involve a fairly low level of personal disclosure and intimacy. (*Example*: Tell how you picked out the person you finally told about the abuse. Why did you choose them?)

RELAXATION TECHNIQUES

Group members practice relaxation techniques for handling high levels of anxiety. These include rehearsal of deep breathing exercises, practice in visualizing a safe, idyllic place, and practice with a simple hand-held galvanic skin response machine which gives an auditory feedback indicating tension levels.

These exercises are focused on helping the group members find ways of handling their anxiety-provoking memories and mastering some of the anxiety aroused by them. The relaxation exercises are followed by "chants" and "cheers."

DIDACTIC DISCUSSION MATERIAL

The discussion of didactic material is centered around insuring future safety, learning how to handle suspicious situations, understanding the causes of sexual abuse, and handling angry feelings about the abuse. Listed below is an outline of topics covered in these discussions.

Insuring Future Safety. The topic is introduced by reminding the girls that young people cannot be expected to automatically know how to protect themselves from abuse. "That was then but this is now. You can learn to protect yourself from future abuse." Then the girls are asked to make lists of answers to the question, "What sort of people should you be suspicious of?" The girls in this instance listed the following:

1. Someone who wants to be alone with you a lot.
2. Someone who is always wanting to have secrets with you.
3. Someone who is always talking about "sexy" things that don't seem quite appropriate.
4. Someone who is always wanting to give you gifts and things which seem very expensive, personal, or more expensive than he gives to others.
5. Someone who is always finding excuses to touch you, or be very close to you in a way that makes you uncomfortable.
6. Someone "hanging around" when you are dressing or in the bathroom, or who seems overly interested in your clothes, hygiene, and so forth.
7. Someone who acts "different" when he is drinking and says and does things when he is drinking that make you feel uncomfortable.
8. Someone who wants to take pictures of you in bathing suits, nightgowns, or have you pose in unusual ways.
9. Someone who wants to discuss sexy magazines, pictures, or television shows.
10. Someone who wants to discuss "growing up and knowing about men," or who wants to help teach you about sex and being married (outside of a class with other children where this information has been approved and monitored).

A number of girls in several groups added that they were especially anxious when fathers or father figures had been without opportunities for sexual contact with their mothers. They felt that when their mothers were ill, hospitalized, away from home for long periods, or working on separate work shifts from their husbands, these men might more readily turn to the young girls in the home for sexual gratification. At any rate, they felt much less protected from sexual overtures in these situations where their mothers were essentially absent from them and their father or father substitute.

How to Handle Suspicious Situations. After group discussion and input, role-play is used to rehearse the following alternative behaviors:

1. Finding ways to avoid being alone with possible abusers, particularly in the situations which had been described previously. Planning activities which kept the girls around other people, and letting their mother know that they felt uncomfortable being left alone, were rehearsed.
2. Role-playing and rehearsing giving an emphatic, "No . . . that makes me uncomfortable and I don't like it!" in a variety of situations.
3. If the potential abuser did not respond, escalating methods of dealing with the behavior were rehearsed, including (a) having each girl develop lists of people she would tell about the situation, (b) practicing calling social services departments and 911 numbers, including listing what information to give on the phone, and (c) hitting, shoving, and running from persons who continued to make advances, and deciding where they would run for immediate help if they needed immediate protection.

Understanding the Causes of Sexual Abuse. The group is asked to make lists of the ideas they have about reasons for someone's becoming a sexual abuser. In early phases of the group, many members tend to include myths and fears about their own behavior or appearance which they feel might have precipitated overtures from the abuser. The areas and questions that seem most difficult for the girls to grasp and understand fully are questions such as: How could a person who seems good in many ways also be a sexual abuser and hurt the same person for whom he had done good, normal things? How could a person who seems normal in all other ways do something that is considered so abnormal? How could he hide his abnormal behavior from other people so completely?

In order to introduce this material some Transactional Analysis materials are used. A chart is shown illustrating how a personality is divided into Child, Adult, and Parent parts, and how these "parts" are stored within us, almost like a "tape" of behaviors and feelings that we use to plan and operate in our everyday lives.

The leaders explain that, "We all operate by using our different tapes, depending on the situation, and on how strongly and how often that tape seems to control a whole personality." The girls are able to relate to the concept that a defective child or parent tape might lead to problems that would interfere with "adult" functioning. Then experiences that might be related to defective functioning in the area of sexuality are listed, including early experiences where the abuser may have been himself a victim of sexual abuse, when early sexual experiences were allowed and encouraged by his childhood environment, or where an abuser may have had early sexual experiences and satisfaction at an inappropriately early time in his own childhood, developing a deviate pattern of sexual ideas and practices.

Poor self-concept and its relation to fear of adult sexuality failure is discussed as another possible factor in child sexual abuse. Lack of effective impulse control, particularly when combined with substance abuse, is noted as another factor. Finally, we consider a simple, sociopathic orientation where a person without a good conscience does not care about another's feelings or needs, and is concerned only with his own immediate satisfaction.

Each girl is asked to identify which issues seem related to her own abuse experience, and to indicate which factors seem to explain some of the causes of the behavior of the person who abused her. An emphasis is placed on understanding that the abuse resulted from the abuser's abnormal sexual behavior, rather than from any provocation or seductive behavior on the girl's part. They are told that understanding the causes of sexual abuse does not excuse the abuser from some type of consequences for the abuse. If abusers will not seek help for their behavior through therapy and other programs, they will need to be separated from society in order to protect other children.

In addition to dealing with some myths that tend to form guilt feelings within the abused girls (e.g., that they had seduced the abuser; that if they were good girls, they would not have been chosen for abuse; etc.), some of their confusion about any pleasant feelings from the abuse is addressed. They are told that, "Some pleasant feelings from the physical part of the sexual abuse might happen. This is a natural thing and something you do not have to feel guilty about. However, the good feelings do not make up for the confusion, anger, and mixed-up feelings that abused children have to deal with both during and after the abuse, and this is why it is not good for an adult to do these sexual things to a child."

Handling Angry Feelings about the Abuse. The girls are asked to list the ways they handled their angry feelings about the abuse before coming into the group, and to decide how effective these were. Most girls list behaviors such as solitary crying, outbursts at their mother and other people, destroying objects in their room, and so on.

Relaxation exercises, thought-stopping techniques, and chants and cheers are discussed as alternative methods for dealing with angry feelings. To encourage more active steps in anger reduction, three exercises are introduced. In the first exercise the girls role-play a situation in which they confront their abuser with a list of questions and a list of the feelings that they want to express. The leaders perform an "alter ego" function similar to psychodrama exercises. They stand behind the players, and remind and encourage them to verbalize as many feelings and issues as possible.

In a second exercise, members are asked to write a letter to their abuser, verbalizing their feelings, reactions, and questions. The members are reminded that the abuser may or may not understand his own behavior and motivations for the abuse. The girls are helped to understand that the abuser may not have the sensitivity and understanding to respond completely to their concerns or statements. However, most abusers should be able to understand to some degree that they have caused pain, harm, and confusion.

A third exercise consists of imagining themselves as being "20 years old, with your own job, maybe your own husband, being completely independent, and feeling good about yourself and how you are doing in life. Pretend that you go back to your old home, and find your abuser there. Tell him about your present life, how you have overcome the abuse, and how well you are doing. Then tell him about the difficulties and suffering he caused you as a child. Then tell him anything else you want from your standpoint as a successful, happy adult person."

GRADUATION AND FOLLOW-UP

At the end of the sessions, a graduation "party" is planned and each girl is given an elaborate certificate, describing her graduation from a "Moving On and Getting Stronger" group. Following the group sessions, each girl receives a monthly "newsletter" for 3 months containing some "reminders" about the material covered in the groups, and telephone numbers of the therapists and social workers she might contact if she has new or increased concerns or problems.

Some girls' groups have chosen, as part of their graduation, to make a videotape or audiotape which is to serve as an introduction for the members in the groups following them. In the tapes they are asked to list the mistaken ideas they had about sexual abuse before coming into the group, to list some of the particular things they liked about the groups, to list some of the ways they felt they were helped by the group, and to make some specific suggestions to the new members about how they can get more out of the groups.

SUMMARY

In this specialized, short-term treatment group for sexually abused, young adolescent girls, group interaction is structured by using a number of original materials such as the "Moving On and Getting Stronger Game," and "Wouldn't It Be Nice" booklet, along with role-play and other structured exercises. Use of these techniques appears to lower anxiety connected with the discussion of difficult, sexualized topics. The materials also allow rehearsal and repetition of the concepts that may be necessary for mastery of responses to abuse. The structured materials also appear to lower anxiety for mothers in the groups and offer valuable information for helping change their own myths and misunderstandings about sexual abuse. In summary, the groups seem to provide a safe and supportive opportunity for mothers and daughters to master feelings and concerns about the abuse.

REFERENCES

Anthony, E. J., & Cohler, B. J. (1987). *The Invulnerable Child.* New York: Guilford.

Berliner, L., & Ernst, E. (1984). Group work with preadolescent sexual assault victims. In I. Stuart & J. Greer (Eds.), *Victims of Sexual Aggression* (pp. 105-123). New York: Van Nostrand Reinhold.

Burgess, A., Groth, N., Holmstrom, L., & Sgroi, S. (Eds.). (1978). *Sexual Assault of Children and Adolescents.* Lexington, MA: Heath.

Corder, B. F., DeBoer, P., & Haizlip, T. (1990). A structured, time limited therapy group for sexually abused preadolescent girls. *Child Abuse and Neglect, 36,* 243-252.

Corder, B. F., & Haizlip, T. (1989). The role of mastery experiences in therapeutic interventions for children dealing with acute trauma: Some implications for treatment of sexual abuse. *Psychiatric Forum, 15,* 57-63.

Pynoos, R., & Spencer, E. (1988). Witness to violence: The child interview. In S. Chess, A. Thomas, & M. Hertzig (Eds.), *Annual Progress in Child Psychiatry and Child Development* (pp. 299-325). New York: Brunner/Mazel.

Rutter, M. (1978). Early sources of security and competence. In J. Bruner & A. Gaston (Eds.), *Human Growth and Development* (pp. 153-188). Oxford: Clarendon Press.

Terr, L. (1981). Psychic trauma in children: Observations following the Chowchilla school bus kidnaping. *American Journal of Psychiatry, 138,* 14-19.

AUTHOR INDEX

A

Anthony, E. J., 125, 140

B

Berkowitz, D., 11
Berkowitz, I., 10
Berliner, L., 140
Bruner, J., 140
Burgess, A., 125, 140
Burroughs, J., 18, 31

C

Canter, S., 3, 11
Chess, S., 2, 11, 140
Cohler, B. J., 125, 140
Corder, B. F., 3, 7, 11, 13, 19, 20, 31, 39, 43, 49, 51, 59, 83, 86, 96, 125, 140
Cornwall, T., 19, 31

D

DeBoer, P., 125, 140
Dick, R., 18, 31
Donahoe, C., 74

SUBJECT INDEX

A

C

M

N

O

P